IDEAS FOR GREAT
WINDOWS & DOORS

Geometrical window wall brings surrounding woods indoors.

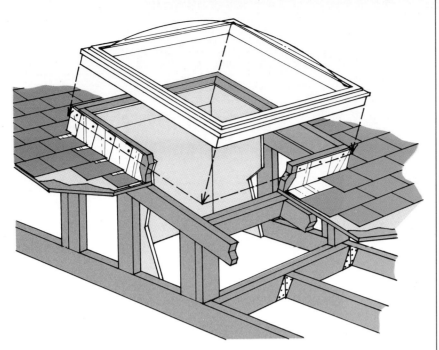

Skylight installation requires framed openings in both roof rafters and ceiling below. For details, see page 21.

Shedding New Light

Low-e glass, pivoting roof windows, and modular, matching door components: these products and more are changing the way we think about residential windows and doors.

This book can show you scores of ways to energize your home, new or old, with openings for daylight, views, and effortless access. Browse through over one hundred color photographs, featuring the latest in products and installations. When you're ready to turn thought into action, we'll help you bone up on current terminology, materials, and planning guidelines.

Many design professionals, manufacturers, and homeowners shared ideas with us or allowed us to photograph their designs. We'd especially like to thank Allwood Door Company, Ashby Lumber, O'Keeffe's Inc., The Pella Window Store, Velux-America Inc., and V & W Patio Door & Window Co., Inc. We'd also like to acknowledge Andersen Windows, Inc., Marvin Windows, Pella/Rolscreen, Wenco Windows, the Vinyl Window and Door Institute, and Alan & Julia Masaoka.

Special thanks go to Rene Lynch for carefully editing the manuscript, and to Brian Pierce for assisting with location photography.

Book Editor
Scott Atkinson

Coordinating Editor
Kathryn Lescroart Detzer

Design
Joe di Chiarro

Illustrations
Mark Pechenik

Photo Styling
JoAnn Masaoka Van Atta

Editorial Director, Sunset Books:
Bob Doyle

Fifth printing October 1999

Photographers: Andersen Windows, Inc.: 29, 30 (top), 36 (left), 57 (top); 87; **Philip Cohen:** 59 (right); **Crandall & Crandall:** 60 (middle and bottom right), 88 (middle left); **Stephen Cridland:** 1, 48 (bottom), 64 (top right); **Fisher Friedman:** 47 (right); **Philip Harvey:** 5, 6, 23, 24-25, 26 (right), 28, 30 (bottom), 32, 33, 34 (right), 35, 36 (right), 37, 39 (bottom), 40, 41, 42 (bottom right), 44 (right), 45 (top left), 45 (bottom right), 46, 48 (top), 49, 50, 51, 52, 53 (bottom), 54 (bottom), 55, 56, 57 (bottom), 58, 59 (top left and bottom left), 60 (left), 61, 63, 64 (bottom left), 65, 66, 70, 71 (right), 73 (top left and top right), 75 (top and bottom left), 76 (bottom), 77, 78, 81 (bottom), 82 (right), 83 (bottom), 85, 88 (top), 89, 90, 92, 93, 94; **House + House:** 60 (top right), 83 (top); **Renee Lynn:** 62; **Marvin Windows:** 31 (right), 88 (bottom); **Terry McCarthy:** 31 (left); **Colin McCrae:** 68, 72, 73 (bottom right); **André Monjoin: 75 bottom right; Don Normark:** 38 (bottom left), 38 (top right), 44 (left); **The Pella Window Store:** 4, 27 (top), 42 (left), 88 (top); **Norman Plate:** 38 (top left), 43, 45 (top right), 54 (top); **Gerald Ratto:** 27 (bottom), 71 (left); **Kenneth Rice:** 81 (top), 82 (top left and bottom left); **Chad Slattery:** 34 (left), 39 (top); **Velux-America Inc.:** 53 (top), 76 (top); **Alan Weintraub:** 26 (left), 31 (left), 45 (bottom left); **Wenco Windows:** 42 (top); **Russ Widstrand:** 47 (left).

Cover: Classic French door ensemble brings light, view, and spring breezes into a bedroom suite. This design combines stock wood unit, overhead fixed arch, and flanking casements. Cover design by Vasken Guiragossian. Photo courtesy of Andersen Windows, Inc.

CONTENTS

SPECIAL FEATURES

WINDOW SHOPPING

Whether you're replacing, remodeling, or building from scratch, the right windows and doors can bring surprising light, efficiency, and personality to your home.

Today's windows come in more shapes and sizes than ever before, and in materials ranging from traditional wood and aluminum to low-maintenance clad wood and vinyl. Gone are the leaky, rattling "guillotines" of the past: now, manufacturers offer classic styling together with the latest energy-saving glazing, frame construction, and hardware. Product lines are often modular, designed for grouping or "ganging" units into one large, exciting statement.

Like Halley's comet, glass block has made another return: use it wherever you need a touch of texture, privacy, or security. Or, for even more pizzazz, look toward stained, leaded, beveled, or etched glass, available either custom or stock.

For sunny accents where you want them, consider the skylight. Pivoting, opening skylights and their

PHOTO COURTESY OF PELLA/ROLSCREEN

Ganged skylights, clerestory windows

ARCHITECT: RAYMOND L. LLOYD. GLAZING: ALAN MASAOKA ARCHITECTURAL GLASS

Decorative window glazing

cousins, roof windows, are blurring the distinctions between traditional units. Flexible skylight placement allows you to paint an interior with light; privacy and ventilation (if your unit opens) are fringe benefits.

Today's exterior doors blend traditional solidity with new insulation and weatherstripping features. For a memorable entry, gang them with matching components—sidelights, transoms, glass block, or decorative glazing options.

When it comes to bridging the indoors with a sunny deck or garden, patio doors are unrivaled. Besides being more handsome and secure than their predecessors, new French and sliding models also feature improved glazing and accessories.

Interior door designs show not only fresh styling but a new function as well. Glazed panels, bifolds, pockets, indoor French doors, or shoji panels all let light pass from space to space, enable you to close off a room for privacy or energy efficiency, or open it completely when sunny weather or a sunny mood dictates. It's like having a great room without the noise or drafts.

With all the choices available, you may be wondering how to get started.

That's where this book can help. It kicks off with a survey of basic window and door options and spells out planning and installation guidelines. An extensive photo gallery follows. If it's product information you're after, see the Shopper's Guide beginning on page 67.

ARCHITECT: REMICK ASSOCIATES. GLAZING: ALAN MASAOKA ARCHITECTURAL GLASS

ARCHITECT: DAVE TERPENING/
CHURCHILL & HAMBELTON ARCHITECTS

French doors, transoms

*Copper entry doors,
beveled glass sidelights*

A PLANNING PRIMER

Whether it's for light, warmth, ventilation, access, or a view, a well-planned window, skylight, or door can have a dramatic impact on your living space.

This chapter explores your choices, walks you through design basics, and outlines the structural realities you'll face. Along the way we help unravel tangled window jargon, show you how to test your ideas, and offer advice on choosing professionals.

You'll find scores of photos and shopping tips in the next two chapters, but use this planning chapter to focus your ideas before you start. Armed with a blend of inspiration and practical know-how, you will be ready to add a beautiful window, skylight, or door wherever you fancy one.

Leaded glass matches original house glazing, brings morning sun and views into remodeled kitchen. Fixed window helps light work area; Dutch doors bridge inside with outdoor deck, provide ventilation in sunny weather.

YOUR BASIC OPTIONS

With so many models and materials to choose from, where do you begin? For starters, it helps to have an overview of the basic types of windows, skylights, and doors available. The following section outlines your basic options; you'll find detailed evaluations and shopping pointers in Chapter 3, "A Shopper's Guide."

WINDOW STYLES

At first glance, the windows in your neighborhood may all look different because of the variety of sizes, shapes, and sash arrangements. But it's likely that they all fall into one of the following categories.

Double hung. Widely used in traditional homes, these units have two sashes—an upper, or outside, sash that moves down and a lower, or inside, sash that moves up in grooves in the frame. The sash movements and positions are controlled by springs, by weights, or by friction devices. Some so-called double hungs are really single hung, meaning that only the bottom sash moves.

Double hungs are prone to air infiltration since most don't seal well. When open, they provide less ventilation and protection from rain than hinged windows. Double hungs may be difficult to clean unless you get a model with removable or rotatable sashes.

Casement. Hinged on their sides like doors, casements are cranked or pushed open, usually outward, for maximum ventilation. Since casements seal tightly, they allow less air infiltration than double hungs.

Most casements available today have an arm's width of space between the opened sash and the frame; this allows you to clean the outside of the sash from the

Basic Window Types

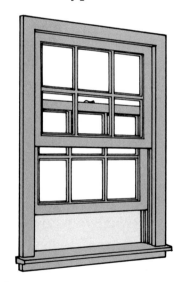

Double hung

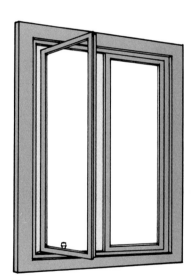

Casement

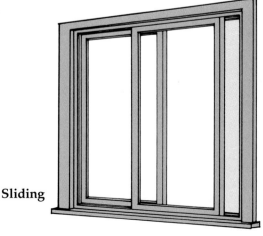

Sliding

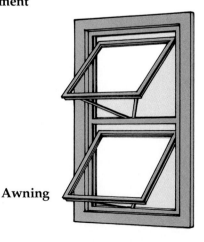

Awning

inside. Pay attention to the opening mechanism: if on a large window the crank pushes only the lower part of the sash, it can eventually distort the sash and prevent a tight closure.

Sliding. This is basically a double hung turned on its side. Sashes slide horizontally in metal or plastic tracks. In the double-sliding variety, both sashes move; in the single-sliding type, one is fixed.

Sliding windows are similar to double hungs in air infiltration, ventilation, cleanability, and cost. However, they don't need the sometimes fickle balancing mechanisms used in double hung designs. Sliders are available in larger sizes, too.

Awning. These windows are hinged at the top and open outward from the bottom. Often they're placed near larger fixed windows for ventilation; they also may be grouped vertically or side by side. The open sash acts like an awning, keeping the rain out. Both sides of some models can be cleaned from indoors.

Hopper. The opposite of awning windows, hopper units are hinged at the bottom and open inward from the top. They're often used in basements where the window openings are at or slightly below grade.

Fixed glass. From expansive picture windows to tiny accents and transoms, these inoperable windows come in many standard shapes, including rectangular, triangular, trapezoidal, semicircular, and elliptical. And if that's not enough, you can usually custom-order the exact shape and size your home requires.

Hopper

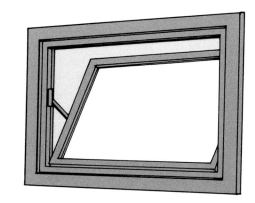

Fixed glass

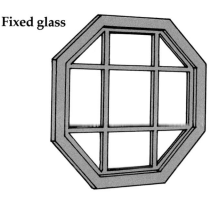

~~

WINDOW WORDS

Strange, intimidating words seem to orbit the subject of windows and their components, construction, and installation. Here's a crash course in standard window jargon, enough to help you brave the showroom, building center, or product brochures. You'll find more information on all these subjects in Chapter 3, "A Shopper's Guide."

Apron. An applied interior trim piece that runs beneath the unit, below the sill.

Casement. A window with a frame that hinges on the side, like a door.

Casing. Wooden window trim, especially interior, added by owner or contractor. Head casing runs at top, side casings flank unit.

Cladding. A protective sheath of aluminum or vinyl covering a window's exterior wood surfaces.

Flashing. Thin sheets, usually metal, that protect window or skylight edges from leaks.

Glazing. The window pane itself—glass, acrylic plastic, or other clear or translucent material. May be one, two (i.e., *double-glazed*), or even three layers thick.

Grille. Decorative, removable grating that makes an expanse of glass look like many smaller panes.

Jamb. Outside frame that surrounds sash or glazing. An *extension jamb* thickens window to match a thick wall.

Lights. Separately framed panes of glass in a multipane window; each light is held by muntins.

Low emissivity (also *low-e*). High-tech treatment sharply improves thermal performance of glass, especially in double-glazed windows, at little added cost.

Mullion. A vertical dividing piece; whereas muntins separate small panes of glass, mullions separate larger expanses or whole windows.

Muntin. Slender strip of wood framing a pane of glass in a multipane window.

R-value. Measure of a material's ability to insulate (retard heat flow); the higher the number, the lower your heating or cooling bills can be.

Sash. A window frame surrounding glass. May be fixed or operable.

Sill. Interior or exterior shelf below window unit. Interior sill may be called a *stool*.

U-value. Measure of the energy efficiency of all the materials in the window; the lower the U-value, the better.

Specialty Windows

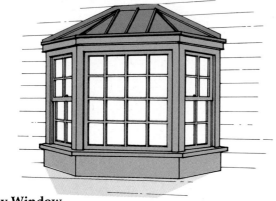

Bay Window

Bow Window

Greenhouse Unit

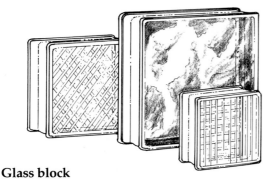

Glass block

Fixed windows are generally the least expensive per square foot, since they have no opening mechanisms. But because they offer no ventilation, they're often used in combination with operable units.

SPECIALTY WINDOWS

When your house demands a sunny breakfast nook, or your A-frame in the country requires a greenhouse unit for plants, you may need to have a window custom-built. But you'll find an impressive collection of creative window styles that you can obtain ready-made.

Bay and bow. These units can open up or expand a living or dining room in dramatic fashion. Some bay installations are cantilevered, furnishing extra sitting or floor space. Typically, you or your contractor add the roof, support framing, and any flooring or seating.

Most bays have one or more straight center windows and angled side windows. A bay with sides perpendicular to the center pane is called a box bay. The windows in a bow curve out, forming a narrow projection in the wall. Bays and bows can consist of fixed or operable windows, or a combination of both.

Greenhouse units. These prefabricated units are small baylike windows designed for growing plants. They come with shelves for pots and planters and are usually made to fit standard-size window openings. Some have sides or tops that open for ventilation. They're favorite additions in kitchens and bathrooms, where moisture, together with the heat and light coming in through the window, produces thriving plants.

Solariums and sun-rooms (page 79) are larger, integral greenhouse options: all have walls, and in some cases they have roofs, made of glass. These porches or rooms usually face south, taking advantage of the sun's warmth.

Glass block. Popular in the 1930s and 1940s, glass block is making a comeback. The reason is simple: besides the decorative appearance, blocks let in soft, diffused light while providing privacy, security, and insulation.

Common block sizes are 6 by 6, 8 by 8, 12 by 12, and 4 by 8 inches; standard thickness for exterior walls is $3\frac{7}{8}$ inches. Units come in such patterns as bubbles, ripples, and swirls. Most block is clear, though Italian block also comes in blue, rose, and green tones, and German block comes in gold tone.

SKYLIGHT STYLES

You might opt for a skylight if, for reasons of security or privacy, the area you want to light cannot have a window; if you live in a row house where the only way to light middle rooms is from the top; or if site exposure or obstructions won't allow much light in through a window.

Manufacturers offer skylights in a variety of shapes, sizes, and glazings and in both fixed and ventilating designs. The roof window is another option for attic spaces or sloped walls.

Fixed skylights. These units range in shape from square to circular. They may be flat, domed, or pyramidal and can vary in size from a skylight small enough to fit between two rafters to one large enough to roof a small room. Several skylights can also be combined to form one large unit.

Skylights with flat surfaces can be glazed with glass or plastic. Domed skylights are always glazed with some type of plastic, a material that molds easily into complex shapes. See page 78 for more information on skylight glazing.

Self-flashing skylights (see drawing at right) are generally for use on roofs with slopes less than 3 in 12 and shingled with thin materials like wood, asphalt, or fiberglass. They are made with both an integral curb and a flange for flashing.

Curb-mounted skylights are used whenever the roof is covered with wood shakes, clay or concrete tiles, or slate, or whenever the slope is greater than 3 in 12. They are designed to be mounted on a wood curb built and flashed by the customer or contractor.

Ventilating units. Most skylight manufacturers offer at least one or two designs that open to allow for ventilation. You can open them either manually with the help of a pole or long cord or automatically using a power unit that works at the touch of a button. Many venting skylights are equipped with insect screens.

Some manufacturers offer motorized skylights and roof sections that can be moved to one side. If you want to open up a room to the night sky, an opening skylight may be the answer.

Roof windows. Think of these rotary units as a cross between windows and opening skylights. They have sashes that rotate on pivots on each side of the frame, which permits easy cleaning and a range of ventilation angles. Unlike opening skylights, they are typically installed on sloping *walls*—such as in a finished attic, or wherever else you can reach them.

Basic Skylights

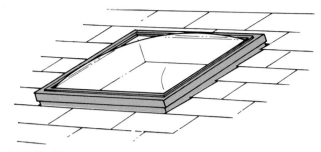

Self-flashing

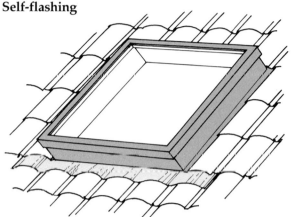

Curb-mounted

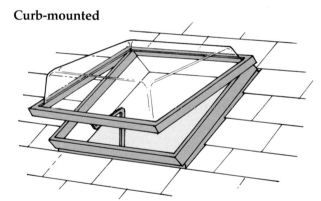

Ventilating Unit

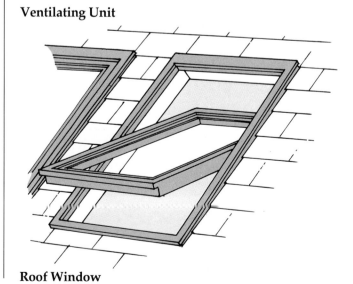

Roof Window

Exterior Door Types

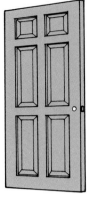

Panel

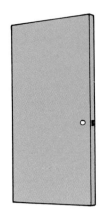

Flush

Double doors with sidelights

DOOR DESIGNS
You'll find a large, bewildering selection of doors at most lumberyards and home improvement centers. Many of the choices are esthetic, but be on the lookout for the following door types.

Basic exterior doors. Though exterior doors vary widely in both materials and appearance, they all come in two basic types: panel and flush. Panel doors consist of solid vertical stiles and horizontal rails, with flat or raised panels in between. (For construction details, see page 80.) Most decorative or custom entry doors are panel types.

Flush doors, on the other hand, are built from thin face and back veneers attached to a solid or gridlike hollow core. Solid-core flush doors are most secure. Whether panel or flush, an entry door should be at least 1¾ inches thick.

Door areas containing glass are called *lights.* A "six-light" door, for example, has six glass panes separated by muntins. Sidelights, flat or arched transoms, and decorative glazing such as leaded or etched glass are all popular accents for entries. Some door manufacturers offer a line of coordinated components, allowing you to combine single or double doors, sidelights, and transoms in a variety of ways.

Dutch doors are split horizontally; the two sections can lock together or operate independently. These units don't seal as well as solid doors, so don't use them in exposed areas. However, they're great for a kitchen or living area adjacent to a sunny garden.

Patio doors. French and sliding doors are traditional choices for bridging indoor and outdoor living spaces. Both types double as windows, offering views, light, and ventilation.

Interior Door Types

Panel

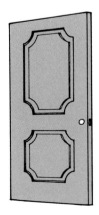

Flush

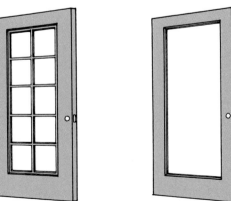

Interior doors with light panels

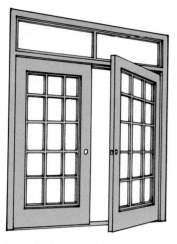
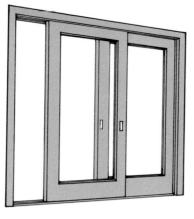

French doors with transom   **Sliding**   **Dutch**

What's the difference? Basically, a French door is a hinged wood door with either one large tempered-glass panel or a number of smaller panes of glass divided by muntins or a grille. These doors usually come in pairs, with an inactive door held stationary by slide bolts at the top and bottom and an active door closing and locking against it.

If you don't have room for a hinged door, then you can opt for a sliding door. Factory-assembled units consist of two-door panels of tempered glass in a wood, vinyl, or aluminum frame. Like a French door, a slider may be purchased with one large glass panel or multiple lights with muntins or grilles.

Interior doors. Again, both flush and panel doors are available for interior use. Doors used inside are often the hollow-core flush type; 1⅜ inches is the standard thick-ness. A traditional or stylized decor may call for a decorative panel door. Small lights or larger glass panels allow an open feel.

If space won't allow a swinging door, consider bifold, pocket, or bypass sliding doors. A bifold door, which runs in a track, is hinged in the middle and folds out. A pocket door slides into a recess in the wall next to the opening. Bypass doors, often used in closets, move past each other in tracks.

Accordion, or folding, doors allow you to tempo-rarily close off one living area from another. Japanese-style shoji panels (see page 62) let soft, diffused light pass between areas.

Self-closing fire doors may be required between any living space and the garage, or for closets containing a water heater or furnace. Check with your building department or fire department for specifics.

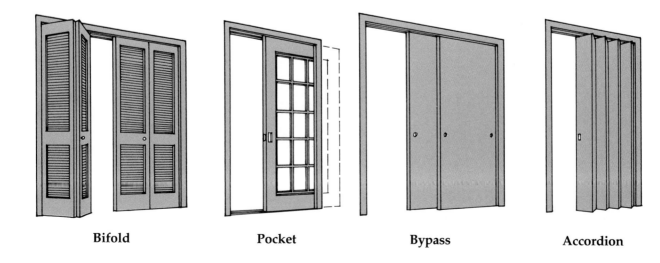

Bifold   **Pocket**   **Bypass**   **Accordion**

PLANNING POINTERS

You'll want to select windows, skylights, and doors that match your home's general style. For starters, study the existing facades. Draw sketches to see how the new addition will affect the building's appearance inside and out. Besides a consistent style, strive for a balanced look. A planning kit or scale model (pages 18–19) can be a very helpful tool at this stage.

Also be sure to check any local codes, ordinances, or homeowner's deeds that may affect your plans. Because of the relative weakness and inefficiency of large expanses of glass, some building codes prescribe a maximum percentage of glass to floor space. You may also run into complications if you plan to remove extensive bracing or sheathing adjacent to a house corner. The moral? Be sure to look before you leap.

WINDOW PLANNING CHECKLIST

In addition to style and appearance, keep in mind several other guidelines when selecting and placing your new windows.

Consider light. The orientation, placement, size, shape, and number of windows will have a significant effect on the amount of light they bring into a room. A south-facing window (north-facing in the southern hemisphere) will let in the most light and is desirable in all but hot climates; a window oriented north provides soft, diffuse light.

The sun also travels from north to south and back again over the course of each year (see drawing below). Permanent or seasonally mounted exterior awnings, canopies, and overhangs are effective for keeping summer sun out while maximizing precious

Plotting the Sun's Path

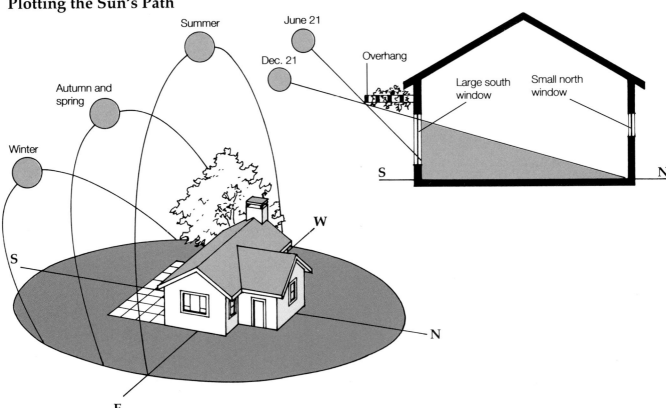

The sun's rays enter a house at prescribed angles, depending on time of year and where you live (above). Large south-facing windows let in maximum light and heat (top right); strategic overhangs or deciduous plantings lend summer shade, admit low winter sun. Small north-facing windows minimize winter heat loss while adding indirect light.

Window Height Guidelines

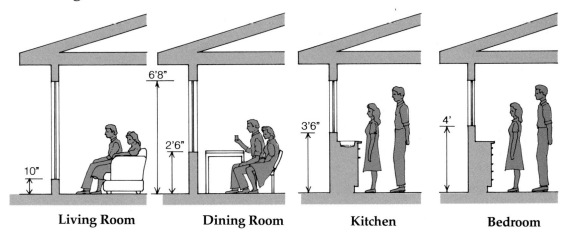

| Living Room | Dining Room | Kitchen | Bedroom |

Plan your windows for easy viewing from standing or seated position. Top height is usually standard; window depth determines sill height.

winter warmth and light. Other options include exterior shutters and other movable shades (see pages 74 and 84).

Light from east- and west-facing windows requires careful management to control its intensity during the summer because of the low sun angles in the morning and late afternoon. To reduce the glare from a tall, narrow window in an east- or west-facing wall, place the window high on the wall to avoid a direct view of the sun, or screen the window on the outside.

Short, wide windows create a broad, shallow distribution of light; tall, narrow windows provide a thin, deep distribution. When you're figuring size, remember that useful light penetrates not more than 2½ times the height of the window. The only way to overcome this limitation is with clerestory windows (see pages 32–35) deep in the room, a skylight, or additional windows on the other walls.

Exterior surfaces adjacent to a window reflect light to varying degrees and can affect the amount of light entering a window. Likewise, reflections from interior surfaces affect the intensity and distribution of light within the room. A white wall reflects as much as 90 percent of the light. Medium tones such as tan, rose, light blue, green, and gray reflect 30 to 50 percent. Dark colors and dark woods reflect less than 15 percent of the light.

What's the view? Of course, you'll want to determine the placement and size of your windows by what you will see from them.

If a spectacular view demands a large picture window, consider breaking up the expanse of glass with muntins. The small panes will create a multitude of framed views while preserving a sense of security and shelter. Some architects recommend several smaller windows instead of one large window; this allows people to catch glimpses of the view as they move around the house.

Ideally, a window sill should be below eye level. But in a kitchen you may want the sill above the level of the counter, in a dining room at about the level of the table, and in a bedroom at about 4 feet from the floor (see drawing above).

If you have a patio, deck, or garden outside a living area or master bedroom, consider placing the sill 10 to 14 inches from the floor (or opt for patio doors). Then you'll be able to see out without craning your neck. Most building codes require the use of tempered glass within 18 inches of the floor.

Standard window height is 80 inches above the floor, matching the tops of doors. This rule is not set in concrete, however, and an occasional small window below this height can be visually effective.

Windows for ventilation. When wind hits the wall of a house, air pressure rises along that wall; on the opposite side of the house where there's protection from the wind, air pressure drops. Windows in these two walls optimize air movement; air coming in through one window and exiting through the window on the opposite wall creates cross ventilation, a relief on warm summer nights.

Study seasonal wind patterns around your house and, if you can, place windows to take advantage of the prevailing breezes.

In summer, some of the cooling effect of air depends on its speed. To accelerate the flow of air through an area, make the window through which air exits larger than the one through which it enters. Also, keeping windows away from corners maximizes air movement.

All but swinging windows open only 50 percent and cannot change air direction, so place them directly in front of the area through which you want air to move. Casements and other swinging windows give you a 100 percent opening; they can be used to direct air sideways, upward, or downward.

Consider privacy. Windows provide light, view, and ventilation, but they also allow others to see inside your home. In addition to using curtains, draperies, and shades for privacy protection, you can plant shrubs or trees outside your windows. Translucent or decorative glazing or glass block serve the same purpose while furnishing artistic accents.

If noise is a problem, both double-glazing and window coverings such as plantings can help reduce it. A short wall, fence, or arbor beyond the window allows light or air in but screens both noise and intrusions.

Think energy. For windows to admit the maximum amount of the sun's heat, they must face south or within 20° east or west of true south. This orientation is essential for catching the winter sun.

When the sun goes down, interior heat is transmitted through the glass to the colder environment. To retard this flow, consider low-emissivity (low-e) glazing (see pages 72–73) or cover the window with insulating material (see pages 84–85).

Another alternative is to let the sunlight fall on material such as brick, masonry, concrete, or water that will absorb and store the heat; after sundown, the material slowly releases its heat into the surrounding environment, keeping the house interior warm. This is known as *passive solar* heating; for more details, see page 79.

Of course, in hot climates you may wish to minimize initial heat gain as much as possible. Again, low-e glass helps retard heat transfer. Other options include interior shutters and shades; exterior shutters, blinds, and screens; sun-control glass and film; and between-the-glass louvers.

SKYLIGHT PLANNING CHECKLIST

A skylight adds light, a view, and in some cases ventilation without affecting privacy or taking up any wall space. With a skylight, you can create an indoor garden and enhance the interior design of your room. When a skylight is properly oriented to take advantage of the sun's heat and is insulated, it can also warm your house in winter.

Skylights for light. All skylights bring in light, but their orientation and glazing affect the quality and quantity of illumination. A south-facing skylight with clear glazing brings in a great amount of light and heat, but it may produce glare. Use it for creating a mood or providing visual interest. The slowly changing beam of light projected by a skylight can provide interest and drama all day.

For soft, uniform light, use a north-facing skylight or one with either translucent glazing or a diffusing panel at the ceiling level.

Light-colored ceiling, walls, light shaft, and furnishings reflect more light, requiring a smaller glazing area for a given lighting requirement.

What's the view? Skylights with clear or tinted glazing allow you to enjoy the view overhead. But remember that, though a view of the trees may be pleasant, putting your unit directly under a tree can present problems, since dirt and debris will collect on it.

Skylights for ventilation. For any area in which you need ventilation, you will obviously select a unit that opens. These units work especially well in bathrooms and kitchens.

You'll also appreciate a venting unit if you live in a warm climate or have a flat-roofed house; when you also open a few windows, opening the skylight at night will allow hot air to escape, cooling down your house.

Skylights and solar heating. When skylights, like windows, are oriented south or within 20° east or west of true south, they admit the maximum amount of the sun's heat in winter. For optimum solar gain, you'll want to tilt the skylight toward the south at an angle of the area's latitude plus 15°. Clear glazing admits the maximum amount of light and heat for the area covered, about 90 percent.

If your skylight is sizable, you may want to shade it either from the inside or from the outside to reduce unwanted solar gain in summer.

Placing a Skylight

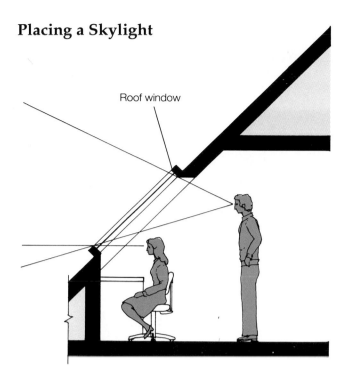

Roof window

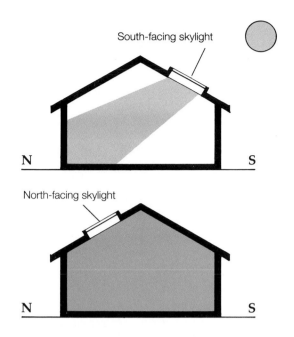

South-facing skylight

N   S

North-facing skylight

N   S

A south-facing skylight (above) admits maximum light and heat; northern exposure provides even, indirect light. When planning a roof window (left), consider the view from both seated and standing positions.

Placing roof windows. There's no hard-and-fast rule for placing roof windows in sloped walls, but window planning guidelines (pages 14–16) generally apply. As a starting point, plan to average out the height between eye level when standing and when sitting. Consider transoms or other fixed panes designed to complement these units.

Light shafts. You'll need a light shaft if there's an attic or crawl space between the roof and ceiling (see drawings at right). In a straight light shaft, the skylight sits directly above the ceiling opening and it is positioned off to one side of the ceiling opening in an angled light shaft. In a flared or splayed light shaft, the ceiling opening is larger than the roof opening; the skylight can sit above or to the side of the ceiling opening.

Sizing principles. A general rule of thumb for determining skylight area is to figure on 1 square foot of skylight area for every 20 square feet of floor space. For example, if your room area is 100 square feet, your skylight area will be 5 square feet. Additional glazing can open up a small room but, depending on the units, may squander energy.

The deeper your light shaft and the higher your ceiling, the larger your skylight will have to be to provide the desired amount of light. But you can bring in the same amount of light with a smaller skylight if you use a light shaft flared between 30° and 60°.

Light Shafts

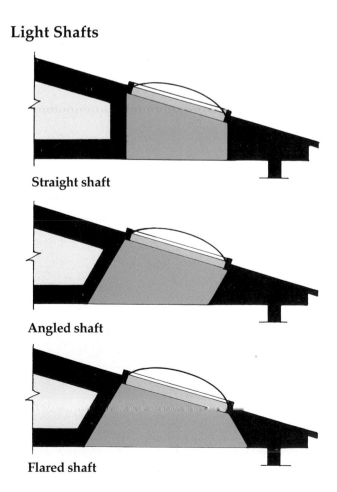

Straight shaft

Angled shaft

Flared shaft

MAKING A MODEL

If we were all designers, there would be no need for the design aids featured below. But the less artistically inclined among us need help in visualizing architectural change. Once you've worked out your ideas with a model, you'll be much more confident about cutting holes in the walls or roof of your home.

Design Kits

Prepackaged kits, the most commonly manufactured design aids, let you arrange scale versions of predrawn interior components on a plan set over a reusable grid. Some packages even help you build a simple model of your project.

Architectural drawing kits contain a series of printed 3-D grids. If you slide these under a sheet of tracing paper, you can draw a room as you'd see it but in correct scale and from a number of different perspectives. You can also purchase a special plastic grid on which you can lay tracing paper and draw straight lines, parallel or perpendicular, every time you put pen to paper.

You'll find an assortment of kits at art and architectural supply stores, at building centers, at some bookstores, and through several catalogs.

Homemade Models

Perhaps the most valuable tool is a small-scale model of your room. Without actually cutting any holes in the walls or roof of your home, you can check the light and view from a proposed window or analyze the quality and amount of light you'll gain from a skylight. Building an adequate model requires only several hours of time and a few dollars for materials.

Make the model from plastic-foam mounting board (available at art supply stores) or balsa wood (try hobby stores). These materials allow you to glue the cutouts back into the walls or ceiling if you change your mind.

You'll also need white glue, straight pins, a ruler, a square, a pencil, and a sharp knife.

Using a scale of ½ inch or 1 inch per foot, draw your floor plan, walls, ceiling, and roof on the building material. Mark all existing and proposed open-

Door Placement Guidelines

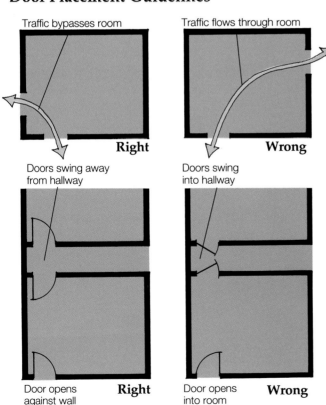

Traffic bypasses room

Right

Traffic flows through room

Wrong

Doors swing away from hallway

Door opens against wall **Right**

Doors swing into hallway

Door opens into room **Wrong**

DOOR PLANNING CHECKLIST
Doors, if they contain glass panels or *lights,* function as windows, too. But there's another list of concerns to tackle: traffic patterns, hinge direction, and, in the case of an exterior door, weather resistance and security.

First, check traffic patterns. Whether you plan an exterior or interior door, determine how it will affect the flow of traffic between the spaces it connects. As shown at left, entry and exit points govern the natural path through a room but strategically placed furniture can help alter this route somewhat.

Which way does it swing? Unless there's a driving reason to position them otherwise, exterior doors should swing inward. Make sure you've allowed wall space where one opens. If door clearance is a problem but you lust for patio doors, consider a sliding unit.

Interior doors usually swing in from hallways. Be sure doors in adjacent walls won't collide when open. Remember that you'll need a wall switch on the nonhinged side of each interior door. In busy

ings. Cut the floor, walls, ceiling, and roof; then cut the window, door, and skylight openings.

With the floor plan as your guide, glue or pin walls to the floor or to each other; then glue the ceiling and the roof. You may want to cut and glue light shaft walls to the opening edges of a skylight before attaching the roof to the walls. If you want to be able to make changes, use the glue sparingly so you can remove and replace the walls easily.

To see how your new opening will alter the light in your home, place your model in direct sunlight, facing in the same direction as your house. Observe the model at different times of day and study the quality and intensity of the changing light. To study the effect of sunlight at different times of year, tilt the model to simulate the change in the height of the sun during the year.

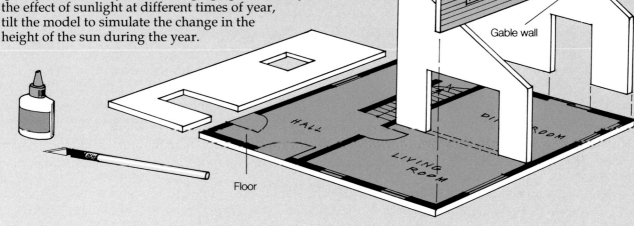

corridors, bifold doors, accordion doors, or doors with tempered-glass panels are safest. Pocket doors are great spacesavers for guest bedrooms, small kitchens, or tiny powder rooms.

Doors for light. You'll find a large selection of single- or multi-light exterior doors available. High transoms add a custom touch to any entry while maintaining privacy. Sidelights can be ganged. French or sliding patio doors are, of course, a classic way to bring the outdoors inside.

Although we commonly think of lights and transoms, we rarely think to use glazing indoors. A glass-paneled door opens up a floor plan while blocking noise and cold air from creeping between rooms. If you need privacy, consider shades or blinds.

How's the weather? An exterior door won't discriminate between you and your guests on one hand and a snowstorm or insect cloud on the other. Ideally, entry doors should be positioned away from the dominant wind and weather direction. The entry should be protected with a roof overhang and rain gutters.

If your door placement falls below the ideal, you can take other steps to minimize the "cold-blast-of-air" or "Niagara-falls-down-the-neck" syndromes. An overhang, pergola, or awning can help. An outside wall can dramatize an entry, screen it from street noise, and block wind and rain from entering. If this is impractical, consider a partial wall inside.

Security. An entry door should be solid and at least 1¾ inches thick. These designs are not only energy-efficient but they help deter forced entry.

Glass panels or sidelights, while attractive, may be security concerns. If located near the lock side, an intruder could simply smash the glass, reach in, and unlock the door from the inside. Consider small, shatterproof glass panels, or substitute glass blocks.

Deadbolts that lock from inside add security, but beware: your family could be locked inside during an emergency. These are banned by some codes. Another option is, of course, a security alarm.

At the front door, you'll want light for safety, security, and decoration. Recessed downlights or an indirect wash from accent lights work well. The only rule is to keep both glare and wattage at a low level.

STRUCTURAL CONCERNS

Whether you're working with professionals or installing a window, skylight, or door yourself, you'll need a basic understanding of the steps involved. The following outlines should give you a feel for each process. If you need do-it-yourself specifics, ask an experienced carpenter for help. For tips on choosing professionals, see the feature box on page 23.

INSTALLING A WINDOW

As shown below, basic window framing consists of a horizontal header, rough sill, and flanking trimmer studs. The header bridges the wall studs on either side, supporting the weight of the ceiling or roof above.

A replacement window that's the same size or smaller than an existing unit can usually be added with minimal carpentry. With new construction, you simply incorporate header, sill, and trimmers into a new stud wall. Remodeling is toughest: before installing the window you must first locate existing framing, remove interior and exterior wall materials between flanking king studs, cut studs as required, and construct the new opening. You'll also need to build a temporary support wall, positioning it about 4 feet away from the existing wall.

Note: Check the area for signs of electrical wiring, water and drain pipes, or heating and ventilation ducts. Any of these obstructions must be carefully rerouted before you remove the wall.

How big should your opening be? Most manufacturers will specify rough opening size, which includes a little slack for sliding the new unit into place and adjusting it for level and plumb. If the unit comes without specs, or you're recycling an old window, measure the outside frame and add about ¾ inch extra to both height and width. Header size is specified by local codes; use a solid beam or build one up from 2-by lumber and ½-inch plywood spacers.

Your window may come with flashing to help seal it against wind and moisture. If not, plan to staple building paper around the opening as shown below. Add a generous bead of caulking compound where window will meet wall.

Window Framing Overview

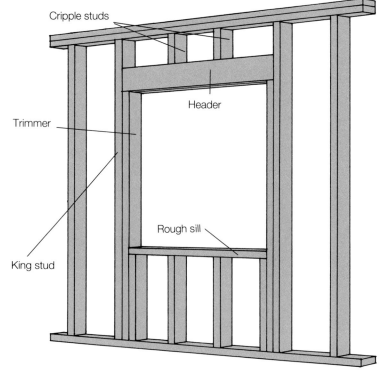

Cripple studs

Header

Trimmer

King stud

Rough sill

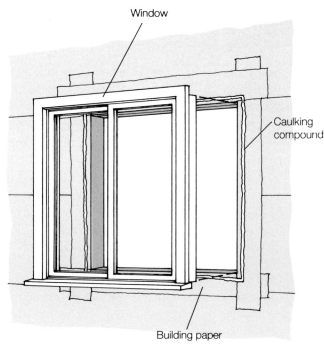

Window

Caulking compound

Building paper

Anatomy of a Skylight

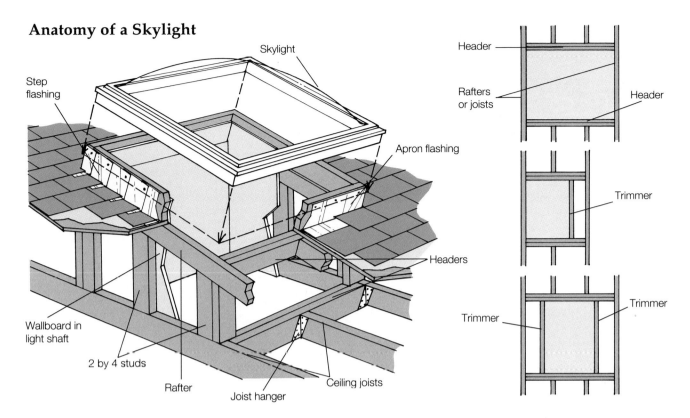

Skylight

Step flashing

Apron flashing

Headers

Wallboard in light shaft

2 by 4 studs

Rafter

Joist hanger

Ceiling joists

Header

Rafters or joists

Header

Trimmer

Trimmer

Trimmer

Following any manufacturer's instructions, level and plumb the window from inside, using wooden shims or wedges. Secure it through exterior flanges, attached trim, or directly through jambs into trimmers and rough sill. Check the unit for smooth operation before driving fasteners home.

Unless your roof has a pronounced overhang, your building code may require an exterior drip cap or head flashing over the new window. Otherwise, simply caulk between the window frame and siding, patch the siding, or add exterior trim as required.

Indoors, stuff fiberglass insulation or foam rope into the spaces between shims. Once interior wall coverings are in place, add interior window trim and break out the paintbrush.

INSTALLING A SKYLIGHT

A skylight's rough opening is much like window framing, except that it's been rotated onto a sloped or horizontal axis. This time, the key structural supports are parallel headers (see drawing above) that bridge rafters or ceiling joists; uncut rafters, joists, or trimmers flank the sides.

Some skylights are sized to slip between adjacent rafters, but many units will require you to cut at least one existing member. Block off any excess width with one or more trimmers, as shown. You'll save

work if you can use at least one existing rafter as a trimmer. Electrical wires or pipes that run through the area must be rerouted before you continue.

It's best to frame the opening from below. Then, on a day with zero chance of precipitation, drill holes up through the roof marking each corner and, working from the roof, cut through the roofing materials and sheathing or decking. When cutting the opening, bridge or brace surrounding rafters or joists. Note: a steep or slick roof is definitely a job for the pros.

Some skylights sit atop a rooftop curb; others have flanges that slide below roofing materials or are secured to the rough framing and covered. Skylights may leak if improperly sealed, so it's critical that you follow manufacturer's recommendations and pay strict attention to any flashing or sealing instructions.

If your skylight must pass through an attic or crawl space, you'll need to construct a light shaft which, as shown on page 17, may be straight, angled, or flared. A ceiling opening is similar to the roof framing, though this time you'll be bridging ceiling joists, not rafters. Frame the light shaft walls with 2 by 4 lumber, as shown.

If your attic is uninsulated, you'll probably want to insulate the light shaft, then finish it with the wall covering of your choice. Finish the skylight by trimming or patching the ceiling opening as required.

Door Installation Overview

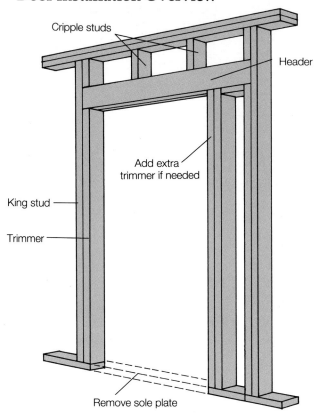

Cripple studs

Header

Add extra
trimmer if needed

King stud

Trimmer

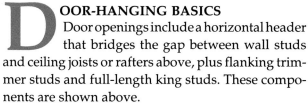

Remove sole plate

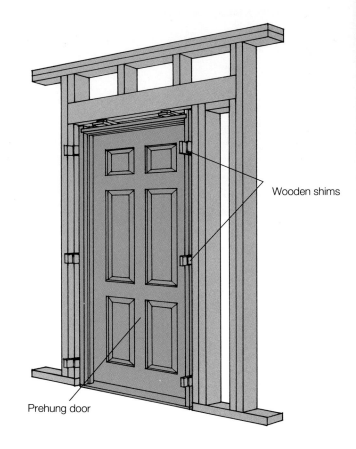

Wooden shims

Prehung door

DOOR-HANGING BASICS

Door openings include a horizontal header that bridges the gap between wall studs and ceiling joists or rafters above, plus flanking trimmer studs and full-length king studs. These components are shown above.

Framing a doorway in a new stud wall is simply a matter of positioning king studs (don't omit any standard studs), then adding header and flanking trimmers. Replacing a door is even easier: at worst, you'll need to remove existing jambs and sill back to the existing framing.

Remodeling is trickier. In existing walls, door framing means cutting through the interior wall covering, removing existing studs and adding new framing, then removing the remaining wall covering or exterior siding inside the opening. If you're placing a door in an existing wall, you'll save work by using at least one existing stud as a king stud. Openings can be blocked down to size with blocking and a third trimmer, as shown. Any existing plumbing or wires must be rerouted before proceeding.

You may need metal flashing above an exterior door; ask your supplier or building inspector. In addition, plan to wrap building paper or plastic "house wrap" around the area.

Prehung doors come hinge-mounted inside their frame or jambs. Typically, you simply slide these into the slightly oversize rough opening, then level and plumb the unit with wooden shims or blocks—as in installing a window.

If your door is not prehung, you have a much bigger job on your hands. You'll need to assemble a jamb set, then secure it plumb and level within the opening. (Add a threshold and/or sill for exterior doors.) Then cut hinge mortises in both door and side jamb and drill for a strike plate and lockset. If you're not up to the detail work, hire a pro.

Even if your door is prehung, it will probably require an appropriate lockset (see pages 83-85). Your lockset kit should include a template for positioning and drilling holes in both doors and jambs.

If you're installing an exterior door, patch the siding, install outside casings as required, then caulk between casing and siding. From inside, stuff foam rope or insulation into the spaces between shims or blocks and finish up with interior casings.

WORKING WITH PROFESSIONALS

The effort you contribute to any project depends on your knowledge, your abilities, your patience, and your health. If you know how to draw up plans but have a bad back, you'll need someone else to perform the physical labor. If you're able to wield a saw and hammer but can't draw a straight line, you may only need professional help to prepare working drawings. Others let professionals handle all the tasks from drawing plans through applying the finishing touches.

No matter whom you consult, be as precise as possible about what you want. Collect pertinent photos from magazines, manufacturers' brochures, and this book. Changing your mind once construction starts usually requires a contract modification, involving both additional expense and delays.

Architect or Designer?

Either an architect or a designer can draw up plans acceptable to building department officials; each can also specify materials for a contractor to order. They can send out bids, help you select a contractor, and supervise the contractor's performance to ensure that your plans and time schedule are being followed. Some architects and designers even double as their own contractors.

Most states require architects to be licensed, but not designers. Many designers charge less for their labor. If stress calculations must be made, designers need state-licensed engineers to design the structure and sign the working drawings; architects can do their own calculations.

Some architects and designers don't charge for time spent in an exploratory interview. For plans, you'll probably be charged on an hourly basis. If you want an architect or designer to select the contractor and keep an eye on construction, plan to pay either an hourly rate or a percentage of the cost of materials and labor—10 to 15 percent is typical.

Choosing a Contractor

Contractors may do more than construction. Often they're skilled drafters, able to draw plans acceptable to building department officials; they can also obtain the necessary building permits. A contractor's experience and technical know-how may even end up saving you money.

If you decide to use a contractor, ask architects, designers, and friends for recommendations. To compare bids for the actual construction, contact at least three state-licensed contractors and give each one either an exact description and sketches of the desired remodeling or plans and specifications prepared by an architect or designer. Include a detailed account of who will be responsible for what work.

Most contractors will bid a fixed price for a remodeling job, to be paid in installments based on the amount of work completed. Many states limit the amount of "good faith" money that contractors can request before work begins.

Though some contractors may want a fee based on a percentage of the cost of materials and labor, it's usually wiser to insist on a fixed-price bid. This protects you against both an unexpected rise in the cost of materials (assuming the contractor does the buying) and the chance that the work will take more time, adding to your labor costs.

DESIGN: RAYMOND L. LLOYD/ROBIN SAWYER
DOOR GLAZING: ALAN MASAOKA ARCHITECTURAL GLASS

Rustic house facade features glazed entry doors and high clerestory windows, providing both light and privacy. Entry was designed in conjunction with architect and decorative glass artist; actual construction was carried out by homeowners.

DESIGN: DIANE STEVENSON DESIGN/DAVID BERKOWITZ. WINDOWS: ALAN MASAOKA ARCHITECTURAL GLASS

WINDOWS
& DOORS
IN ACTION

Whether they
are windows, doors, or skylights, openings
can have an enormous impact on the form
and function of your home. On the following pages, we'll demonstrate many of the
possibilities.

We've shown as wide a range of designs
as possible, from tiny accents to expansive
overviews. Some of these treatments are
classics; others are more innovative.
Although your home may not look like any
of these, many of the ideas are easily trans-
latable.

When plotting new openings, consider
the visual effects both inside and out. Also
review traffic patterns, sun direction, privacy needs, and energy efficiency. (For
help, see pages 14-19.) And don't overlook
the finishing touches, such as window trim
or treatments. For specific shopping tips or
product details, check "A Shopper's
Guide," beginning on page 67.

*Soft evening light plays across
glowing wooden window bays.
Box units feature decorative leaded
glass; they're supported by custom
brackets. While adding light
and views inside, bays form a
repeating exterior accent.*

CLASSIC VIEWS

Casement, double-hung, slider, fixed: when we look out at a great view, it's usually through one of these traditional window styles.

To maximize impact, architects and designers often "gang" several standard windows vertically or side by side; or mix and match fixed and operating units into one spectacular window wall. Most manufacturers offer combination units sharing one top jamb and sill. Some provide hardware for ganging smaller stock units (such as fixed windows, awnings, and elliptical tops) into a creation all your own. Place windows next to patio doors, or mix in stained glass; the possibilities are practically endless.

ARCHITECT: HOUSE + HOUSE OF SAN FRANCISCO

Whether viewed from inside or out, grouped windows become an integral part of a home's design. The sleek breakfast area above features narrow curved panes topped with transoms. Tall aluminum picture windows (at right) strike a strong motif from outside, and allow wide views toward patio and landscape from indoors.

ARCHITECT: CHURCHILL & HAMBELTON ARCHITECTS

Fixed windows at right form a living room window wall, highlighting a 180° forest view; lower awning units open for ventilation. The striking night view below illustrates how grouped window shapes add personality from outside.

ARCHITECT: HOUSE + HOUSE OF SAN FRANCISCO

CLASSIC
VIEWS

Wood casement windows and transoms (right) maintain traditional decor, and were situated to allow full morning sun in the breakfast room. New units below feature "two-way" operation: they open from the side (like casements) for maximum ventilation and to allow cleaning; or from above, as shown.

*Modern double-hung replacement windows frame
an ocean view; they're joined by a fixed pentagon
in the peaked gable wall. Trim divided grilles
snap off for easy cleaning.*

CLASSIC
VIEWS

Living room walls provide special opportunities for window design statements. The stock fixed units shown at right are grouped into a pleasing geometric shape; manufacturer's hardware helps link units. Below, classic gable-wall glazing blends graceful muntin lines with traditional trim.

ARCHITECT: DANIEL W. WINEY

Complex window shapes can be difficult—and expensive—to manufacture and install. Here's one alternative: shape the outside opening as you wish, then recess a more traditional window profile behind it.

Corners also present challenges, and this window offers a novel solution. The seamless corner unit can sit alone, or may be combined with other stock units to continue a view or glazing pattern across adjacent walls.

ARCHITECT: ACE ARCHITECTS

Window walls and glazed doors add exterior drama to this duneside house.
High clerestory windows in the rounded turret announce the entry while
bringing outside light deep into living spaces.

ARCHITECT: BREDTHAUER/CURRAN & ASSOCIATES

HIGH LIGHT

How can you "lift" a view, bring extra light deeper into a room, or combine drama and privacy? Look up!

When normal eye-level windows won't work due to privacy considerations or lack of wall space or views, consider the clerestory. These allow light and shadow to play on adjacent walls and floors in an infinite range of patterns, changing a room's character throughout the day.

Cathedral windows emphasize the sweep of a raised ceiling and high roofline while flooding a space with light. In homes where cathedral or multistory windows are used, rooms on the upper floors often have openings facing them so they can share the light and view.

DESIGNER: MRD DESIGN

An elegant spiral stairway leads the eye up to grouped wood windows above. Multipane fixed units add daytime light and double as view windows from the second-story landing.

HIGH

LIGHT

DESIGNER: ROBIN KERPER

An arched cathedral window (right) brings light to both first-floor kitchen and second-floor bedroom; the custom unit was aimed at a nearby liquidambar tree. Small, randomly placed windows (above) ascend to the vaulted 14-foot roof peak, preserving a reading nook's privacy while filling the room with soft reflected light.

ARCHITECT: MORIMOTO ARCHITECTS

High glazing helps "lift" a room while admitting light deep into a house. Ridgeline and gable glazing (above) brighten a central great room; an eyebrow dormer (below) extends light and view through a dining room, hallway, and into the living room via wall cutouts.

Clerestory windows (above) bring light to a tall family room while allowing unrestricted use of wall space. Clerestories also lift the eye, stretching a room's apparent height.

WINDOWS & DOORS IN ACTION   **35**

POP-OUTS

Bays, bows, and other pop-outs have an almost magical way of expanding both views and interior space. Manufactured bays and greenhouse windows are readily available, or construct your own "sliver addition." For an instant sun-room, consider glazing the roof as well as the sides.

Most pop-outs start with a wide opening cut in an outside wall. Some simply cantilever outward and tie into the existing foundation; others require new foundations tied to the old. Modern cable systems help shore up heavy manufactured units. Floors, roofs, window seats, and trim may or may not be included.

A bay window brings in light while adding an angular exterior accent. The 45° bay above has opening casements on each side. Manufactured units may not include support brackets or roofing materials; this roof is topped with copper, a popular custom touch.

A bow window expands interior living space and adds extra light while maintaining a simple, graceful curve. This manufactured bow adds a subtle counterpoint to the country exterior, while echoing the wavy shingle courses above.

This large bow, adjacent to the living room, serves an "observation deck" function and as a striking accent both inside and out. It's formed from tall, fixed center units and flanking casements; tongue-and-groove cedar lines the ceiling.

DESIGNER: MOLLY RUTH HALE

DESIGNER: MOLLY RUTH HALE

DESIGNER: LINDA BROCK, BROCK BUILT INC.

DESIGN: DIANE STEVENSON DESIGN
WINDOWS: ALAN MASAOKA ARCHITECTURAL GLASS

Small pop-outs add accents and surprising space to remodels. A stock greenhouse unit (top left) expands a small bathroom; a piano bay (bottom left) features private, mirror glazing outside; three sideyard glass block bays (above) provide space for sitting, bathing, and office areas.

ARCHITECT: WILLIAM P. BRUDER

A built-in window seat nestles into the space created by a 90° pop-out; the unit combines a fixed picture window with flanking casement and awning units.

This bathroom bay seems to "float" the whirlpool tub right into the surrounding woods. Decorative window panes help focus windows on trees and screen bathers from outside view.

DYNAMIC ACCENTS

Whether it's called stained, leaded, beveled, etched, or sandblasted, decorative glass can turn a window into a work of art. The glass might be mineral hued, painted, clear, sandblasted, or mirrored. Textures vary from smooth to rough, rippled, or knobby. Beveled edges on clear pieces can break white light into rainbows.

Place decorative windows where they will take advantage of changing light. Set them alone, or combine them with clear glazing to "edit" a view. For extra drama, shoot a light through from outside at night. Although these units are usually fixed, they may be installed in movable sashes—casements are the most popular.

ARCHITECT: FISHER-FRIEDMAN ASSOCIATES

A small, arched casement window adds its accent to the dining room wall and allows a glimpse of outdoor greenery.

ARCHITECT: REMICK ASSOCIATES

Leaded windows introduce circular accents to a traditional dining room. Sections may take a variety of custom shapes; glazing can be clear, diffused, or colored.

...our square, etched windows augment a ...eometrical design found throughout this ...athroom; they bring in light while ...aintaining privacy. The overhead ...kylight adds extra light and interest.

WINDOWS & DOORS IN ACTION **41**

PHOTO COURTESY OF WENCO WINDOWS

Decorative glass is an option on some stock window and door units. The manufactured casements and transom at right combine design flair with solid, modern construction.

ARCHITECT: MORIMOTO ARCHITECTS
WINDOWS: ALAN MASAOKA ARCHITECTURAL GLASS

PHOTO COURTESY PELLA/ROLSCREEN

A dramatic circle window (above) soars high in a gable wall; as a bonus, it opens in the center. Decorative beveled glass (right) offers a striking counterpoint to the built-in window seat and flanking cabinetry.

Don't forget the design possibilities of strong window trim. Here, square panes and colorful frame and muntins enhance the sense of enclosure in the sitting area while showcasing the view.

ARCHITECT: WILLIAM R. DUTCHER

43

PRIVATE LIGHT

When a bathroom, bedroom, or other living space faces the street or the neighbors, sometimes it's best to trade a little light for privacy.

Glass block or decorative glass—stained, sandblasted, or beveled—all can provide a decorative flourish while maintaining a reserved exterior. Each is available in a wide variety of finishes. If you wish, scatter a few clear sections among the translucent ones, allowing insiders a view but preventing passersby from seeing in.

Glass block has additional merits around an entry: it's more secure than a regulation window or sidelight, and it provides better insulation.

DESIGN: CYNTHIA SNELLMAN PRICE

ARCHITECT: REMICK ASSOCIATES

To block an unwanted view without shutting out all light, the homeowner had the window between a utility room and entertaining kitchen sandblasted. This is custom work: you can either prepare your own design using masking tape, or the sandblaster will work out a design with you.

Glass block is tailor-made for bathroom installations, enhancing the sense of space while maintaining privacy. This glass-block grouping brings soft light to a walk-in shower.

A curved shower wall (above) has glass block below, clear glazing at eye level. The bathroom dormer below provides room for a walk-in shower; clear blocks offer discreet views out.

Frosted bay glazing (top) provides an elegant backdrop and soft light while ensuring a private soak. Above, a bedroom's glass block wall offers a clear, "edited" view out while masking streetside views in.

SKYLIGHT STRATEGIES

Nothing puts light where you want it like a skylight. Flat, bubbled, or peaked, fixed or opening, a skylight can range from a tiny accent that brings a shaft of light along the wall to an imposing arched roof vault to multiple roof windows.

Skylight effects hinge on size and placement, but also on glazing. Choose from glass or acrylic in clear, tinted, or energy-efficient versions. Light shafts help aim or spread daylight; for soft, even light, consider a diffusing panel at ceiling level.

Unfortunately, light-bringing skylights may become black holes at night. For a dramatic effect, how about placing light fixtures inside the light shaft or above a ceiling panel?

DESIGNER: GEOFFREY FROST/
KITCHEN STUDIO LOS ANGELES

Skylights may add welcome light and views during the day, but they become dark holes at night. This light well houses an attractive pendant fixture that solves the problem and provides a focal point for the kitchen below.

ARCHITECT: FISHER-FRIEDMAN ASSOCIATES

A sloped attic space is a natural for an artist's loft studio, and venting skylights are a natural glazing choice. These units not only yield inspirational views over neighboring trees; opening sashes also vent creative heat.

A roof vault forms the striking centerpiece of this two-story entry foyer; it also sheds light on surrounding wings. Frame and ribs are aluminum; bronzed acrylic glazing helps reduce direct solar gain and blocks UV rays. Skylights this size are custom-fabricated.

SKYLIGHT
STRATEGIES

ARCHITECT: RAYMOND L. LLOYD

Skylights help illuminate areas that really need it. The fixed skylight panels at right lead the eye up and out past roof trusses, shedding light on the center of a large living room. Pivoting roof windows (below) help light— and vent—a busy kitchen sink area.

ARCHITECT: JERRY WARD, WARD ARCHITECTURE PC

DESIGN: DANIEL W. WINEY/CHERI VARNUM

Skylights also help jazz up a cramped or boring ceiling. A small bedroom (right) is stretched and brightened with high, fixed glass panels. The great room below is glazed with large expanses of diffusing acrylic; individual "skylights" are formed by floating ceiling trim.

ARCHITECT: BREDEHAUER/CURRAN & ASSOCIATES

SUNNY SPACES

From greenhouse sections to one-of-a-kind spaces, sun-rooms or solariums make dramatic spots for sitting, sunning, or dining. You can take two main routes: a prefabricated unit or modular kit or walls and roof assembled from stock windows, skylights, and patio doors.

Sun-rooms are great for auxiliary heating. In a passive solar system, you can store heat by letting sunlight fall on brick, concrete, or water that will absorb and store the heat; after sundown, the material slowly releases its heat into the surrounding environment.

A sun-room can produce too much heat and glare, especially in summer, so movable window insulation and mechanical ventilation may be required in warm climates.

This sun-room links first- and second-story living spaces, ganging a window wall and French doors below its unique glazed roof. A trap door leads to the roof—and to a handy hose for rinsing off the glass.

This two-story window wall, flanked by glazed doors, forms the multipaned centerpiece of an entrance hall and allows sun and views to flood both the main floor and an upstairs landing.

ARCHITECT: CHURCHILL & HAMBELTON ARCHITECTS

ARCHITECT: HOUSE + HOUSE OF SAN FRANCISCO

The formal English sun-room was prefabricated in Europe and shipped in pieces; the structure nests into a former "L" in the house exterior. Ceiling fan, motorized window shades, and mechanical vent system help cool both the household cat and its owners.

Sun-rooms can serve as transition zones while providing light and views. An expanded entry room (right) combines glazed walls and movable roof with handsome fir doors. Matching sets of arched doors (below) provide the elegant link between a formal living room and the landscape beyond.

ARCHITECT: CHURCHILL & HAMBELTON ARCHITECTS

ARCHITECT: CHURCHILL & HAMBELTON ARCHITECTS

In contrast to custom fabrications, you can also "build" a sunspace from stock glazed units. The living room at left gangs standard windows and doors with multiple skylights. Glass block adds spa-side privacy to the garden room below.

ARCHITECT: HOUSE + HOUSE OF SAN FRANCISCO

A classic living room window wall below links inside to outside via French doors, tall windows, and graceful dormer. The deckside design at left goes one step further: this wall opens up completely to the garden beyond.

BRINGING THE OUTDOORS IN

One of today's favorite remodeling strategies is to "stretch" interior space with a patio or deck. French or sliding doors help link living space and garden while doubling as view walls.

You might gang French or sliding units with other doors or matching windows. Look overhead for transoms, awnings, or hopper units. Some manufacturers offer sidelights to match their doors; or add tall, flanking casement windows.

If you live in a mild climate, there's another option: tall, movable door panels that slide on tracks. On sunny days, these can open a living space or sun-room completely to the elements.

ARCHITECT: GEORGE BROOK-KOTHLOW & ASSOCIATES

The view toward a springtime scene leads through informal wood-and-glass doors and flanking sidelights; seamless corner glazing presents an unobstructed view. A small skylight tops off the assemblage.

BRINGING THE
OUTDOORS IN

In temperate climes, why not open up the wall to summer weather? The pool house below features "removable" walls—solid fir doors that telescope on triple sliding tracks. At right, a remodeled suite utilizes a standard garage door and hardware to open up a sitting area to surrounding hills.

ARCHITECT: CHARLES DEBBAS

ARCHITECT: MORIMOTO ARCHITECTS

PHOTO COURTESY OF ANDERSEN WINDOWS, INC.

Bright red bifold doors (below) evoke Southwestern openness, provide garden access to an open floor plan's central hall. A standard option, the sliding patio door (right), solves door-swing problems, stays weathertight, and looks great, too.

ARCHITECT: ACE ARCHITECTS

ELEGANT ENTRIES

First impressions are lasting ones, and your front entry makes a statement about you and your house. Do you prefer single or double doors? Standard or tall? You'll find a huge selection of both stock and custom units to choose from. Add sidelights, glass blocks or leaded accents, maybe an overhead transom. Consider the effects both inside and out.

Besides welcoming guests, an entry should offer shelter from rain and wind, admit light, and maintain a semblance of privacy. It's fun to plan a striking design, but don't forget security (see page 19). Efficient but glare-free light fixtures provide both safety and design accents after dark.

A classic entry door and overhead transom open onto a Georgian entry hallway. Interior doors and transoms spread light to flanking parlors, too.

ARCHITECT: DAVE TERPENING/
CHURCHILL & HAMBELTON ARCHITECTS

Dramatic entrys mean more than just doors. The formal arched opening at left reveals a view over the sunken living room, to an echoing arched transom beyond. Oxidized copper, beveled glass, and crisp interior lighting team up to make a memorable interior (below left).

Arched dutch doors (above) blend graceful lines with a comfortable, informal ambience. On sunny days, split doors allow views, light, and garden surroundings to enter the house beyond.

59

Entry doors preview unique homes. The etched door at top right is inscribed with the architectural plan of the house within; it glows invitingly at night. The double doors at center are recycled from an old elevator. The frosted doors shown at bottom feature four matching bevels.

ARCHITECT: MORIMOTO ARCHITECTS

ARCHITECT: HOUSE + HOUSE OF SAN FRANCISCO

ARCHITECT: POWELL DESIGN GROUP

DESIGN: CALVIN L. SMITH ASSOCIATES, INC.

A custom entry door (left), crafted from vertical-grain fir, is flanked by matching sidelights, previewing this home's quiet but elegant Japanese design.

This unique entry opens to the back, not the front of the house, allowing owners and guests to enjoy the rear garden while dining. Double-glazed doors and transoms are joined by custom corner windows, maximizing garden views.

WINDOWS & DOORS IN ACTION **61**

Shoji panels function both as interior doors and as movable wall sections. For company or an open floor plan, simply slide them open on telescoping tracks; for privacy, shut them down. Most shoji panels are built from vertical-grain fir or Port Orford cedar.

INTERIOR DOORS

Sometimes a standard flush door is just fine, but there are other options—from traditional double parlor doors to discreet pocket doors, from arched to curved shapes. Door hinges and hardware help customize any selection.

Interior doors needn't be impenetrable barriers. Single- or multi-light panels admit sunshine and views while sealing off noise and drafts; frosted or diffused panels extend privacy.

Flexible, track-mounted shoji panels or movable screens are another option: close them down for solitude; open them up for entertaining or for letting in good weather.

ARCHITECT: BREDTHAUER/CURRAN & ASSOCIATES

Pocket doors offer a clean, uncluttered solution to door-swing problems and clearance headaches. This door looks arched, but it's not: the rectangular fir door simply slides in an arched opening. It's the curved door rail that creates the illusion.

Interior doors help connect rooms as well as seal them off. The French doors above link a sun-room with adjacent living quarters, bringing a glimpse of outside through two rooms. The hallway passage door at left partitions off a shower room, but elegant frosted glass lets soft outside light enter.

ARCHITECT: CHARLES DEBBAS

All lines lead to a matched pair of swinging doors, which blend decorative German glass with trim deco styling. These arched frames swing within their arched opening, sealing a guest suite from the adjacent house.

ARCHITECT: THE SCHUTTE HAYES GROUP

A SHOPPER'S GUIDE

By now, you should possess a new appreciation for how windows, skylights, and doors can enhance your home's style and efficiency. The next step is getting down to business by hitting the pavement. But before you do, take the time to read through this chapter.

Here you'll learn what's available in the marketplace, where to shop, how to compare similar products, and what questions to ask. Think of this material as basic preparation for the enticing sights in the window or door showroom, building center, or lumberyard.

You'll also find tips for adding interior window treatments, shopping for sunrooms, and making existing doors and windows more energy-efficient. To help you locate many of the products you need, pages 94–95 list information sources.

Custom steel windows lend geometrical motif to this receding passageway, bringing sunlight and garden views to a bedroom wing. Steel frames blend strength with trim muntin lines; their clean appearance harmonizes with many contemporary designs.

67

WINDOWS

Among the myriad of window styles available are (1) primed wood casement with simulated divided lights, (2) wood slider with aluminum cladding and snap-on grille, (3) prefinished wood casement, (4) anodized aluminum slider, (5) vinyl double-hung, (6) wood circle with aluminum cladding, and (7) aluminum octagon.

If you're in the market for new or replacement windows, you're in luck. Manufacturers offer literally thousands of variations, from arched casements and old-fashioned bays to hinged or sliding styles, all with a dizzying assortment of framing and glazing options. If the window you want isn't standard, many manufacturers will make one to your specifications.

Shopping Pointers

Windows are sold through many sources, including manufacturers, name-brand dealer networks, window stores, home centers, and lumberyards. Take the confusion out of the buying process by deciding first on the style of the window you want, then the frame material, next the accessories, and finally the glazing.

If you're switching to a different style or size, be sure to check local codes before buying; codes specify ventilation requirements and often insist on enough open window space for access by firefighters. Also, energy codes govern the percentage of glass-to-floor area.

Look for a solidly constructed window with strong, tight joints and smooth operation. Sashes should open easily and close flush all around, and window locks should shut securely without undue force. Each pane should be fully sealed in the sash, and weatherstripping should provide a continuous seal around the window.

If low maintenance is important, consider a frame that needs little or no care. Some manufacturers offer hardware designed to withstand moisture and salt air.

Before choosing a window, consider how easy it will be to clean. Some double-hung models allow you to remove the sash from the channel. Newer casement windows have sliding pivot arms so they can open several inches in from the corner, allowing you to reach the outer pane.

Ask about options such as removable panes, integral miniblinds, or pleated shades (see page 73), hardware colors, and screens. Are the screens easy to operate? Do they obscure the view or window styling?

Prices vary depending on the window type, framing material, glazing, and options. Good-quality, standard-size double-hung and sliding windows cost roughly $8 to $14 per square foot with single glazing and $11 to $17 per square foot with insulated glass. Standard-size casements and other hinged types cost roughly $16 to $22 per square foot with single glazing and $19 to $28 for insulating glass. Low-e glass (see pages 72–73) is standard with some companies and costs up to 20 percent more with other companies. Custom sizes cost up to twice as much as standard-size windows of the same type.

Installation charges vary from area to area. It costs more to install odd-shaped windows, since additional framing is required.

Energy Efficiency

Soon all windows will be marketed with labels listing their U value—the rate of heat flow through the window—in accordance with a uniform energy rating system developed by the National Fenestration Rating Council (NFRC). Until these ratings appear, ask for the window's U value (rather than the R value, which relates to a material's resistance to heat transfer). Make sure the value you get is for the whole window and not just the glass.

The lower the U value, the more energy-efficient the window. A window with a U value of 0.2 to 0.3 is considered very good, 0.4 to 0.6 average, and 0.7 or more poor. The colder your climate, the more important a low U value; in a warm climate, an average U value is fine.

Divided Lights

Divided-light windows, which have several individual panes, are good-looking and traditional, but they're costly and inefficient, since they lose

COMPARING WINDOW FRAMES

Wood

Advantages. Wood is traditional, natural, durable, and insulating. Windows can be ordered bare, primed, or prefinished.

Disadvantages. Because wood swells with moisture, wood frames can stick. Wood windows need regular refinishing and can rot if not properly maintained. Paint buildup can make windows hard to open and close, and can lead to air infiltration.

Cost. Initial expenditure depends on quality and whether the wood is finished. Upkeep adds to the cost.

Clad wood

Advantages. Wrapping wood with a thin layer of vinyl or aluminum eliminates exterior maintenance problems while retaining good insulation.

Disadvantages. The inside surface must be refinished periodically. The outside color is permanent and the color choices limited, typically white and a few shades of brown and gray. If you want another color, you may have to buy paintable cladding. Rotting is possible under the cladding.

Cost. Clad wood costs about 20 percent more than bare wood and about the same as prefinished wood.

Aluminum

Advantages. This strong, light material is more likely to keep its shape than wood or vinyl. Anodized or color-bonded aluminum is virtually maintenance-free.

Disadvantages. Aluminum is subject to nicks and scratches. Without a thermal break (a layer of nonconducting material), the frame will transmit heat. Still, most thermally broken aluminum frames aren't as energy-efficient as other types of frames. For this reason, aluminum is used mainly in mild climates.

Cost. Aluminum windows range from about half as much as premium wood windows to about the same price.

Vinyl

Advantages. Vinyl without steel reinforcing is as energy-efficient as wood, and new insulated vinyl can be even more efficient. Since vinyl has a permanent integral color, scratches can't lead to corrosion. Many improvements have made quality vinyl frames more suitable for all climates.

Disadvantages. Vinyl frames are usually available only in white or beige, since dark colors absorb too much heat.

Cost. Vinyl windows can cost as much as premium wood windows, but they're not as inexpensive as low-end aluminum windows.

Steel

Advantages. Steel has a modern, clean look with narrow framing lines, allowing maximum visibility. Extremely durable, today's steel windows have maintenance-free factory finishes.

Disadvantages. High cost is the biggest drawback. Although less conductive than aluminum, steel isn't as energy-efficient as other framing materials. Double-hungs and sliders aren't available.

Cost. The most expensive material, steel becomes more competitive when used in curved, odd-shaped, or very large windows.

Fiberglass

Advantages. More insulating than wood, fiberglass is strong and durable. Windows come with a white or brown polyurethane coating that can be painted.

Disadvantages. Fiberglass windows are so new that long-term performance is unknown. (The windows debuted in the Northeast in 1990 and will gradually become available nationwide.)

Cost. Prices are comparable to those for premium wood windows.

Angled wood windows nestle around a stone fireplace and chimney, providing novel views from a cozy living room. Hearth-level casements continue the design and allow ventilation.

energy from the edges of each pane. They also weaken a window with large expanses of glass.

For a similar look that's more energy-efficient and less expensive, you can opt for a grille that snaps into holders on the frame, adheres to the surface of the glass, or fits between double glazing.

For a more authentic appearance, choose simulated divided lights, formed by metal spacers or foam strips placed between double-glazed panes with wood muntins glued to the glass on both sides. You'll pay more for these, which are called *true divided-light* windows.

Ordering & Taking Delivery

You need to provide the supplier with the height and width of the window openings and the thickness of the wall. Most firms will send a representative to your house to take measurements and discuss options, but sometimes this happens only after you visit their showroom.

If the window style you want isn't available off the shelf, ask about delivery time. Some manufacturers don't stock all the sizes they offer but build them to order, which can delay a remodeling job considerably.

Ask for a written warranty and note exactly what's covered by the manufacturer and for how long a period of time. Be aware that if you install the windows yourself, you may invalidate the guarantee. Make sure to check new windows thoroughly before accepting them.

ARCHITECT: JON SATHER ERLANDSON

Anatomy of a Window

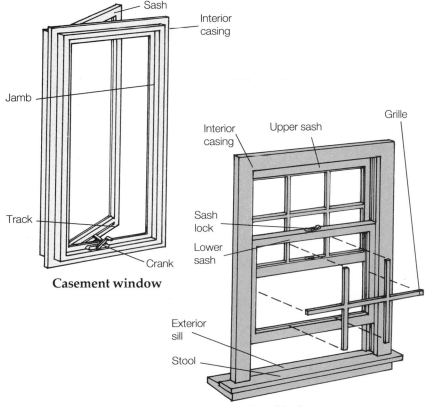

Casement window

Double-hung window

Aluminum window walls were a striking but economical choice for a budget-minded home design. Because of thermal-break construction, these ganged units help save energy, too.

Fixed steel windows flank a steel door, provide a sunny southern view at the end of narrow house wing. Steel windows are available custom only; while beautiful, they can be quite costly.

ARCHITECT: THE SCHUTTE HAYES GROUP

Glazing Options

Many of the greatest strides in window technology are taking place in glazing. Among the newest products are double-paned glass that turns at a 90° angle and liquid-crystal-laminated glass that changes from opaque to clear when an electrical current runs through it.

Manufacturers have pushed hard to improve energy efficiency. A major breakthrough is a glass system with an R-8 value (R value is resistance to heat flow), which insulates twice as well as the most efficient glazing previously available.

But don't buy a window based just on the glazing's R value, since the glass often outperforms the window frame. When shopping for windows, the crucial figure is the U value (see page 69).

What you should expect from window glass depends largely on where you live. In a cold climate, you want glazing that lets in plenty of solar energy, yet allows little heat to escape. In a warm climate, controlling heat gain is key. In any climate, the glass should reduce condensation, cut fabric-fading ultraviolet light, and be as clear as possible.

Before choosing glass, contact your local building department to find out what type of glazing the energy code in your area recommends.

Types of glass. Here are the main kinds of window glass used in homes.

■ *Flat glass* is ordinary window glass (⅛ inch is standard for homes). This glass can be strengthened, coated, and tinted.

■ *Insulating glass* is made of two or more panes of glass sealed together, with a space between the panes to trap air. Whether it is worthwhile to have double or triple glazing in your windows depends on the climate and heating costs in your area.

Sometimes a break in the seal can develop. The best warranties cover a new window and installation if the seal fails within 10 years.

■ *Laminated glass,* a shatter-resistant safety glass, consists of two panes with a middle layer of polyvinyl butyral (PVB). If the glass breaks, it crumbles into small chunks, which adhere to the

Low-e Heat Transfer

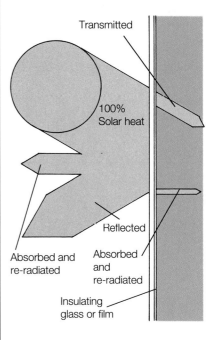

Cross-section of insulating glass (left) shows two panes separated by a hollow aluminum tube in the frame. Air trapped between the panes acts as an insulator. Low-e coating (above) deflects outside ultraviolet rays while retaining indoor radiant heat.

Double glazing allows internal mini-blind (left) and pleated shade (below) options. They're operated by discreet hardware on the window frame.

laminate. Laminated glass also helps block noise and ultraviolet light.

■ *Tempered glass,* also a safety glass, is shatter resistant and heat resistant; it's two to five times stronger than ordinary glass. If tempered glass breaks, it breaks into pieces, not shards.

Glass treatments. Glass manufacturers have devised a number of treatments to control unwanted heat gain or loss.

■ *Tinted glass,* usually bronze, gray, or greenish blue, is suitable for warm climates or unprotected southern or western exposures, where it can lower air-conditioning costs by blocking solar heat gain. The ideal tinted glass has a low-shading coefficient (heat blocking) and a high daylight transmittance (pleasant light inside and a clear view outside).

■ *Reflective glass,* used mainly in commercial buildings, stops more solar heat gain than any other treatment. However, the view from inside is obscured.

■ *Low-e, or low-emissivity, glass* usually consists of two sealed panes separated by an air space and a transparent metallic coating. The coating is either suspended in the air space or applied to one of the glass surfaces facing it. For single glazing and unsealed double-paned units, a coating can be fused to the glass during production.

Nearly as clear as untreated glass, low-e glass insulates a window and deflects the sun's ultraviolet rays. But its chief virtue until recently—blocking indoor radiant heat from escaping—has made it practical mainly in northern climates.

Now, spectrally selective coatings, which reduce solar heat gain without darkening the glass, are making low-e a desirable choice in milder climates. This new type of low-e glass is expected to replace tinted and reflective coatings as the preferred way to reduce heat gain.

Some manufacturers combine low-e glass with argon, a colorless, odorless gas pumped in and sealed between double panes to add extra insulation. The gas improves thermal performance by about a third over standard low-e models at little added cost. Low-e glass with argon nearly doubles the insulating ability of dual-pane glass.

Window screening for blocking insects and solar rays is available in assorted colors and mesh sizes. Darker screen colors obscure less of the view.

THE WORLD OF WINDOW TREATMENTS

Although most windows stand on their own merits, sometimes conditions such as decor, sun, or the need for privacy call for special window treatments. Here's a look at five basic options: curtains, draperies, shades, shutters and screens, and blinds.

Curtains

Once curtains were considered strictly casual, but they have now earned a place in even the most elegant interiors. That's not to say that informal curtains are relics of the past; rather, the choices and treatments are now wonderfully varied, from short cafes to billowy floor-length panels, from simple gathered headings to tabs and ties.

By definition, curtains are either gathered on a rod or attached to a rod by tabs, rings, or ties. If the curtains open and close, it's done by hand.

If you lack the time, desire, or budget for a custom-made window treatment, ready-to-hang curtains or draperies serve your purposes handsomely. They're sold in department stores, home furnishing stores, specialty shops, and mail-order outlets, and usually, the supplier also carries the hardware you need for hanging them.

Linings increase the life of the curtains, reduce noise, block light, and add insulation. Lined curtains have more body and hang better than unlined ones, and they also look better because, in most cases, the hems don't show from the front.

Draperies

Draperies used to be staid and predictable: pleated panels hanging from hooks attached to narrow traverse rods. But not anymore. A wealth of trims, new varieties of hardware and fabric, and imaginative applications of headings have enlivened this traditional window covering, making possible intriguing, even surprising, effects.

Choices in drapery fabrics have multiplied. Sheer fabrics filter daylight and give some daytime privacy, but at night you may want something heavier. Casement fabrics are traditional choices; like sheers, they soften a window but generally give greater privacy at night. Medium-weight and heavy fabrics lend a formal, classic look and provide good insulation, light control, and night-time privacy.

Lining drapery fabric protects against fading, adds insulation, and makes the draperies look fuller and hang better. An interlining sandwiched between the drapery fabric and lining provides even more insulation.

Shades

From tailored roller and Roman styles to frothy Austrian and balloon creations, shades are as versatile in use as they are varied in style. They provide privacy, block light, and conserve energy.

Although shades that roll up or draw up in tidy or billowing folds are still very popular, innovative high-tech styles are making inroads in the market. New styles include pleated shades with an insulating honeycomb design and shades that roll up but have fabric slats that tilt like Venetian blinds to control light.

Roman shades draw up into neat horizontal folds, Austrian shades into scalloped folds, and balloon shades into billows. All have rings on the back through which cords are strung.

Shutters & Screens

In some situations, hard-edged treatments such as shutters and screens lend elegance, simplicity, and architectural interest to a room. When they are closed, solid-panel shutters block all light; louvered shutters, lattice screens, and the delicate Japanese shojis allow varying amounts of light to enter.

Traditional shutters have 1¼-inch louvers set in panels approximately 8 to 12 inches wide. Plantation shutters have wide louvers—most commonly 2½ to 4½ inches—set in panels roughly 15 to 36 inches wide. Wide louvers offer more ventilation and a clearer view than narrower ones.

Blinds

Although they differ in appearance, all blinds have slats that compactly stack up or off the window's glazing and tilt for privacy and light control.

With their sleek, hard-edged appearance, blinds are appropriate in most contemporary schemes, but they don't absorb much sound and, with inside mounts, complete darkening may not be possible.

Venetian blinds, the original horizontal blinds, have 2-inch-wide slats held together by cotton tapes or nylon cords. Miniblinds, an updated, pared-down version of Venetian blinds, have 1-inch metal or vinyl slats that tilt when you turn a wand. Miniblinds come in a wide range of colors and patterns.

Vertical blinds have all the advantages of horizontal blinds as well as the side-draw operation of draperies. Their wide slats can be made of PVC, fabric, wood, painted aluminum, or polycarbonate plastic; some slats have grooves for wallpaper or fabric strips to match or complement walls or furnishings.

DESIGN: CORINNE WILEY, ASID

Window treatments can add beauty and flexibility to sunny window walls. Pleated curtains (above) are held back with brass medallions to permit a full view. Plantation shutters (below) invite the outdoors in, joining interior and exterior spaces. Roman shades and vertical blinds (right) help screen a sun-room section.

DESIGN: JANICE M. STEIN, VILLA INTERIORS

SKYLIGHTS

PHOTO COURTESY OF VELUX-AMERICA INC.

Skylights can bring light deep into a room and create a sense of drama where there was merely a blank ceiling before. But some versions have also gained a nagging reputation for trouble, such as leaks, condensation, or heat loss. If you shop for a quality skylight, however, and have it installed correctly, you should find that these rumors are unfounded.

Shopping Pointers

You can purchase skylights at the same outlets as windows: specialty showrooms, home improvement centers, and some lumberyards. Ask about energy efficiency, frame materials, light transmission, and reliability. Have there been any leaks reported? Will there be condensation or moisture running down the wall or ceiling? How tricky is the installation? Be advised that if you plan to install the skylight yourself, your warranty could be voided.

Make sure that you have the right design for your situation before buying. Curb-mounted skylights are typically used whenever the roof is covered with heavy wood shakes, clay or concrete tiles, or slate, or whenever the roof slope is greater than 3 in 12. They are designed to be mounted on a wood curb built and flashed by the customer or contractor.

Ganged skylights combine light-gathering efficiency with novel design possibilities. Curb-mounted units (bottom) are set in deep wells, help light dining and kitchen areas. Bedroom (top) benefits from electric opening units with sun-control blinds.

ARCHITECT: GEORGE CODY/CODY ASSOCIATES

Pyramid-shaped bubble skylight teams up with a small accent window to carry light and warmth to a basement office. The pyramid shape was molded in one weathertight piece, then "frame" lines were added for accent.

Self-flashing skylights are for use on roofs with slopes less than 3 in 12 and shingled with thin materials like wood, asphalt, or fiberglass. They are made with both an integral curb and a flange for flashing.

You can pay as little as $100 for a fixed acrylic skylight, about $500 for a pivoting model that you crank open with a pole, or several thousand dollars for a motorized unit that automatically closes when a moisture sensor detects rain. Flashing and other installation hardware will be extra, as will any add-on accessories.

The world of custom skylights is almost as unlimited as the world of custom windows. Most large manufacturers will design and make a skylight that meets your special needs.

Curb & Frame Construction

Most skylights are made of wood, clad wood, or aluminum. In coastal environments, you may want to give further protection against salt spray by painting the frame.

Some manufacturers use urethane, fiberglass, or even wood—all good insulators—for the curb in self-flashing skylights. Others insulate a metal frame with wood or plastic foam to provide a thermal break. Skylights with thermal breaks made of insulating material lose less heat through the frame and don't suffer from condensation on the metal surfaces.

Skylight types include bubble-shaped curb-mounted (1); flat self-flashing (2); and trim venting model (3) with integral curb.

A few manufacturers offer skylights made of molded clear plastic. The plastic extends into a flange that's secured directly to the roof deck and covered with shingles.

Glazing Options

Skylights may be single-, double-, or perhaps even quadruple-glazed. Though a single-glazed unit will work in temperate climates that require neither heating nor air conditioning, use a double-glazed unit at the very least in all other climates. The dead air space between the glazing layers (see photo at right) acts as an insulator and reduces heat loss or gain to a considerable degree.

In an extremely cold climate, you can obtain extra insulation in a skylight by using a triple glazing, but at considerable expense.

Glass is used only in skylights with flat glazing surfaces. Because it's brittle and cracks and breaks if struck, most quality skylights are fitted with safety glass. In some areas, tempered glass is required on the outside and laminated glass on the inside; if the tempered pane breaks, the laminated one will prevent the glass from falling. Laminated glass also greatly reduces ultraviolet rays. Generally, glass is more expensive than plastic.

Acrylic is standard on less expensive models and on curved skylights. Ultraviolet stabilizers have extended the life span of acrylic to about 20 years.

Glazing colors for plastic have traditionally been transparent gray or bronze, translucent, and clear, but a variety of decorator colors, both transparent and semiopaque, are also available.

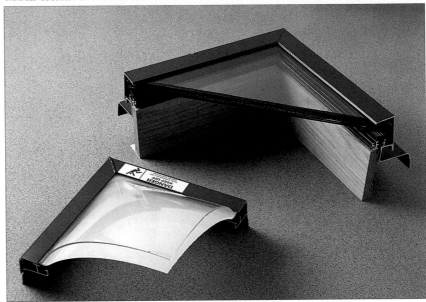

Basic skylight glazings include molded acrylic (bottom left) and low-e glass (top right). Both samples feature double glazing.

Flashings for curb-mounted units include standard galvanized saddle and step pieces (left), and color-matched, fitted components (right).

Though clear plastic glazing admits the most light and heat (ideal for solar heating purposes), it may cause glare and a spotlight effect unless oriented to the north. If it's insulated, it will show the condensation that may form between the layers.

Translucent glazing diffuses light, spreading it evenly in an interior space. Bronze and gray glazings significantly lower glare and the incoming amounts of light and heat.

Hardware Options

Screens are usually included with operable skylights, and some companies offer miniblinds or shades. You can also install a motor unit and matching wall switch to operate a rooftop model.

Besides add-on features, you should also determine what installation hardware is required for your new skylight. Curb-mounted skylights require a wood curb, typically 2 by 6 construction lumber. The curb is covered with metal flashing (see photo on facing page), either specially manufactured or standard galvanized steel. Your supplier should stock the correct type for the job. Don't substitute a different flashing: not only may your warranty be canceled, but the skylight will probably leak.

Many skylight manufacturers shy away from endorsing flat-roof installations. If you do wish to install a skylight on a flat roof, be sure to discuss this with your supplier. To encourage drainage, slope the curb a minimum of ¼ inch per foot, or use the manufacturer's flat-roof curb and flashing kit, if available.

If you plan to group or "gang" several skylights, ask whether or not the manufacturer sells special connecting hardware and flashing for this purpose.

SHOPPING FOR A SUN-ROOM

Sun-room, solarium, conservatory, greenhouse section, sun porch: these are all names for a popular glazed room addition. A sun-room can be incorporated into a new home or added to your present one. It can be built from stock windows, doors, and skylights; custom-designed and fabricated; or purchased in modular kit form. A sun-room brings a bright, cheery environment to your home year-round; combined with a thermal mass, it also helps heat your house in winter or at night.

Design Guidelines

A sun-room is designed to retain sun and heat, so first it should face south—or within 20° of true south. Second—nothing should block the sun when it dips to its lowest winter path.

The structure may either adjoin a living area directly or—more effective in hot climates—be isolated from the main house. This so-called buffering allows you to insulate the inner, or north, wall and to tap warm air from the sun-room at your discretion.

To maximize heat-absorbing surfaces, or thermal mass, incorporate brick, tile, or other masonry units; poured concrete; or even water storage tanks into interior walls or floor. These materials absorb heat during the day, then slowly release it at night.

Of course, all that heat can fry you in summer, so any sun-room requires venting at times. Options to consider include ceiling fans, opening roof sections, mechanical vents, ducting, and power-operated shades or sensors.

Shopping Tips

If you're in the market for a sun-room, you have three basic options: to assemble one from stock windows, skylights, and/or French doors; to custom-design one; or to purchase a kit from a sun-room dealer.

A do-it-yourself sun-room is usually the least expensive option. Window and skylight manufacturers often sell hardware allowing you to "gang" multiple units together. Some window dealers will help you design a sun-room from scratch.

You can also hire an architect or designer to design the structure and a contractor to install it. This is a more expensive route, but you'll benefit from their expertise and have some recourse in case of leaks or other structural problems.

Or you can shop locally for a prefabricated sun-room. Check the yellow pages under "Sun Rooms, Greenhouse & Solarium Builders" for leads. Ask about options in both framing and glazing. Is condensation a problem? Is the structure finished inside? Shop around for an established dealer—one who will be there to service the unit, if necessary. Five years is a standard warranty period.

Some kits are relatively easy for an experienced do-it-yourselfer to install; others are thornier. If you're trying to decide whether or not to tackle the job, here's a tip: ask to see the printed instructions before you buy.

In any case, you'll probably need to start with an existing or freshly poured concrete slab and footings. You'll also need to determine whether your proposed design, kit or custom, will pass local energy and structural codes.

EXTERIOR DOORS

An exterior door has a tough life. On the one hand, it represents you and your family to the outside world. On the other, it must stand up to whatever the elements wish to throw at it, while continuing to look great and work smoothly. This need for both form and function makes careful shopping important.

Shopping for Doors

You'll find standard exterior doors at lumberyards, home centers, and specialized door retailers. Most home centers are geared for hands-on appraisal, allowing you to shop by eyesight, not from a catalog's pages. However, the selection can be spotty, and quality may be a notch below other sources. Door specialists know what's available and what works. If you're after a period look, a salvage yard may offer interesting recycled doors. But beware: if you take this route, you're accepting the blame for improper hanging or leaks.

You can buy doors loose or prehung (see page 83), in kit form, single or double, and coordinated, if you wish, with matching sidelights, overhead transoms, and decorative glass.

Whatever door style you opt for, ask these basic questions: How is it constructed? What joinery is used? Will it warp? What maintenance is needed? Is it well insulated? Does it open and close smoothly? Is there a tight seal all the way around? What options are included? What finish does it need? Don't forget that you'll see it from inside, too.

You or your dealer will also need to determine some basic specs that determine your door's fit. What's the rough opening? How thick is the wall? Which way will the door open? What hinges and hardware are required?

Ask about the warranty and determine exactly what it covers. If the door is to be delivered, check the unit carefully before accepting it.

Construction Basics

Standard exterior doors are either panel or flush, with or without glazed openings or lights. Standard entry door height is about 78 inches, standard entry door width is 36 inches, and typical thickness is 1¾ inches. Auxiliary doors may be 32 inches wide. All of these dimensions are flexible, especially if you go the custom route. The market is aimed at replacements for existing doors, so chances are good that you can find what you're looking for.

Traditional panel doors have hardwood rails and stiles (see drawing above left); panels are either flat or raised, built from plywood or solid lumber sections glued up from smaller widths. Ask about joinery. How are rails or stiles joined? Are panels floating or fixed?

Exterior Door Details

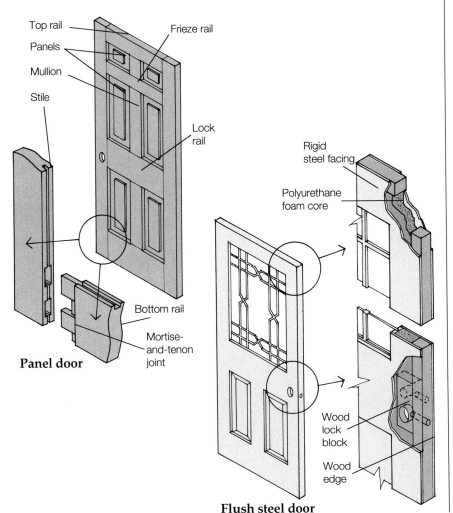

Panel door

Top rail
Panels
Mullion
Stile
Frieze rail
Lock rail
Bottom rail
Mortise-and-tenon joint

Flush steel door

Rigid steel facing
Polyurethane foam core
Wood lock block
Wood edge

Stock door lineup (below) features, from left to right: insulated steel construction with half-round transom; frame-and-panel fir with glazed lights; classic raised panel; and solid-core flush door with birch skin. Front entry (right) combines optional sidelights, transoms, and glazed double doors into one striking ensemble.

A SHOPPER'S GUIDE **81**

Traditional doors can provide inspiration for modern construction. Two ancestors at left show colorful Mexican detailing; custom flush door (below) is a modern descendant. Arched opening adds depth and interest to new entry.

ARCHITECT: CHURCHILL & HAMBELTON ARCHITECTS

Flush doors are *sandwiches*, built from a core material covered with plywood, hardboard, or another material to be stained or painted. For both security and insulating reasons, the core should be solid, not hollow like an interior door.

Door exteriors may be wood, or wood clad with either vinyl or aluminum, fiberglass, or, increasingly, steel. Insulated cores, excellent weatherstripping, and the lack of wood movement make steel doors especially weathertight. And don't rule them out from an esthetic standpoint: simulated raised or recessed panels have the look of the real thing, with extra strength, security, and fire resistance built in.

Of course, there's also a whole world of custom doors, allowing you to choose both design and wood species. Just remember that weight and wood movement are the checkpoints to consider.

Prehung or Separates?

You can buy exterior doors separate or as part of an ensemble line featuring sidelights, transoms, and hardware. Prehung units are particularly good for exterior applications: otherwise, you'll need to add hinges, lockset, threshold and/or sill, and weatherstripping yourself, dramatically increasing the odds for trouble.

Door specialty yards can prehang the doors and accessories of your choice for you, then deliver them as a single unit ready to install. For installation basics, see page 22.

Lockset Logic

Popular exterior locksets fall into three basic types: cylindrical, mortise, and deadbolt. Each type is shown on page 84.

Cylindrical locksets, commonly found in houses built since about 1960, are operated by a key inserted into the exterior knob; the interior knob is operated either by a small push or turn button on the knob or by a key inserted into it. Tubular locksets are similar to

DESIGNER: MRD DESIGN

Novel hardware helps put a custom stamp on entry doors. Wrought-iron handle and deadbolt (left) are interior part of mortise lockset; striking vertical handles (above) are hardworking towel bars adapted to new duty.

A Look at Locksets

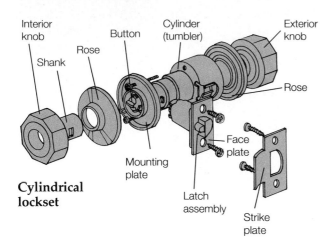

Interior knob · Shank · Rose · Button · Cylinder (tumbler) · Exterior knob · Rose · Face plate · Mounting plate · Latch assembly · Strike plate

Cylindrical lockset

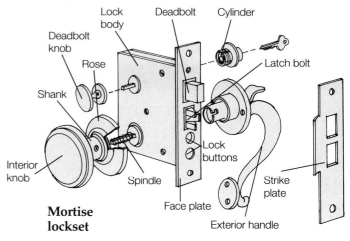

Lock body · Deadbolt · Cylinder · Deadbolt knob · Rose · Latch bolt · Shank · Interior knob · Spindle · Lock buttons · Face plate · Strike plate · Exterior handle

Mortise lockset

ENERGY SAVERS

Most new windows and doors are engineered for weathertightness and energy savings. But a number of strategies will improve the odds, especially if you're living with old, less-than-seaworthy units.

Reducing Heat Gain

In summer, excessive heat gain through windows can be a problem, especially in rooms that face south or west. The most effective way to reduce heat gain is to stop the sun's rays outside, before they get to the glass. Interior treatments allow some heat to enter, but they may be more convenient to use than exterior treatments. Both approaches will, unfortunately, block light and obstruct the view.

■ *Awnings* help keep indoor temperatures down by shading windows. The amount of heat reduction depends on the direction the window faces and the color of the awning fabric. Some awnings can be retracted from the inside; others, sensing the sun and wind, open and close automatically.

■ *Solar screens* effectively reduce heat gain by shading windows. Exterior shades offer the best protection. Lightweight screens of woven fiberglass mesh block the sun but allow breezes to enter. Heavier screens of vinyl-coated polyester fabric are best on windows where the sun is constant. For even more protection, choose louvered aluminum shade screens.

Interior screens, opaque or semisheer, are somewhat less effective, but they're practical because they're easily raised and lowered from the inside. Draperies, vertical blinds, or roll-up, Roman, or pleated shades make soft screening.

■ *Solar control film* is coated with microscopic metal particles on one side and adhesive on the other. The film comes in various colors, from slightly to heavily tinted. In a southern climate, choose a standard solar control film, which can block about 60 percent of the sun's heat. In a more moderate climate, a less heavily metalized film is a better choice; use it where you want to cut glare and fading more than heat.

Low-e film, designed to be similar to low-e glass (see pages 72–73), allows solar heat to enter and prevents much of the radiant heat from escaping.

Up to 4 mils thick, *safety film* strengthens glass and holds it together if it breaks. It's available clear or with a reflective coating.

Check with the supplier to make sure your windows are suitable for window film. You can install film yourself, but it can be tricky to do it without leaving bubbles or trapping particles underneath.

Preventing Heat Loss

In addition to effective window coverings, a number of energy-saving treatments and strategies keep the interior of your home warmer in winter.

■ *Weatherstripping* helps shore up existing window and door openings against cold air and dampness. For weatherstripping under doors, there are *thresholds* and *door bottoms, sweeps,* and *shoes*. Sealing the edges of doors and some windows calls for *jamb weatherstripping*.

Installing weatherstripping is usually easy: in most cases, you need only a few common household tools and the patience to align and fit the pieces

cylindrical ones but have smaller, weaker locking mechanisms.

The one-piece body of a mortise lockset is set into a large, rectangular recess in the edge of the door. The lockset has one or two lock buttons in the face plate and usually has a deadbolt that double locks the door, as well as a spring-loaded thumb latch on the exterior handle. They're considered more secure than cylindrical locksets but are less popular because they're tougher to install.

For real security, there's no substitute for a separate deadbolt. For best security, it should have a 1-inch throw.

So-called double-key deadbolts are sometimes installed where there's adjacent door glass. These prevent a burglar from reaching in and opening the lock from inside, but can present a hazard during a fire or other emergency. Double-key units are illegal in some areas.

In older homes, you might find rim locks, which are surface-mounted and originally operated with old-fashioned iron keys. To locate these, check mail-order catalogs and renovators' supply houses

To choose hardware, you'll need to provide your supplier with some

basic information about your door. First, is it a right-hand or left-hand door? "Hand" is determined from the outside; a left-hand door is hinged on the left, a right-hand door on the right. You'll also need to know the door's thickness, the width of the stile (especially for a mortise lock), and the backset (the distance from the edge of the door to the center of the knob hole).

If it's an existing door, check the hole size or mortise size and the lockset brand presently in place. Better yet, take the current lockset with you when you shop. You *can* change brand name or lock type, but it's not always easy.

properly. You may have to trim a door, either to make room for the weatherstripping or to get the door to fit properly.

■ *Caulking* helps seal cracks and joints between exterior casings and siding, or between adjacent sashes, mullions, or panes of glass.

Caulking is simple and relatively inexpensive, and it can cut up to 10 percent off your heating bills. Apply it with a caulking gun or putty knife. Silicone caulks last longest, but they are tricky to paint over.

■ *Insulation* is often inadequate or missing. Many older windows and doors are improperly sealed around the edges or between jambs and wall framing. To check, gently remove exterior or interior casings.

Foam rope, available in coils from hardware stores or building centers, or polyurethane foam in cans fill gaps too large to caulk. For big holes, stuff in strips of fiberglass insulation, reapply the casings, and caulk their edges.

Door- and window-sealing products abound at hardware stores and building centers. Weatherstripping, caulking, and insulation products head the list.

PATIO DOORS

Think of patio doors as "windows you can walk through." They have similar glazing and grille options as windows, and they present many of the same construction problems and solutions. But you'll also need to determine how these units perform as hard-working doors.

Shopping for Patio Doors

Window showrooms usually stock patio doors, too—and some home centers are now carrying better wood, wood clad, and vinyl lines as well as traditional aluminum.

So-called French doors come in two basic versions: hinged and sliding. Hinged doors are traditional but require space for door swing and can be tougher to weatherstrip effectively. Modern sliders look much like hinged doors and offer several plusses: they won't require space for door swing, they seal tightly, and it's easy to incorporate a sliding screen door into the works. One panel is stationary, the other slides.

Patio doors are available in a variety of widths; 80 inches is the standard height. A "standard" width is 6 feet, though smaller models—as low as 5 and even 4 feet—are available from some manufacturers. New versions are often sold as replacements for aging aluminum sliders, and they come in corresponding sizes.

Like window lines from the same manufacturers, you can add a host of accessories to your basic door unit, such as overhead transoms, fixed sidelights, or casement or awning windows above or to the sides.

When sizing up your choices, you'll need to determine door swing direction or slide direction (both specified as you're facing the unit from outside), plus wall thickness. Architects and interior designers love French doors to open out, but door installers don't: these models are tough to weatherproof.

Materials & Construction

Like windows, patio doors are available in wood, wood clad, vinyl, aluminum, and steel (custom only). For material comparisons, see page 69.

Wood clad is a popular choice, combining the traditional wood feel and look inside with a tough, maintenance free exterior. Ask about your cladding options: What colors are available? Can you paint over it? Be sure to seal any unprimed surfaces immediately, before installation.

Vinyl doors are tight, smooth, and nearly maintenance free and won't swell and contract with weather like wood can. Today's aluminum sliders, outfitted with energy-efficient glazing, effective weatherstripping, and thermal breaks, are greatly improved.

Patio Door Components

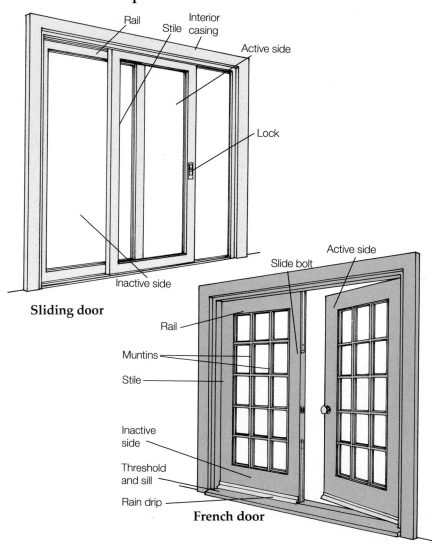

Rail
Stile
Interior casing
Active side
Lock
Inactive side
Sliding door

Active side
Slide bolt
Rail
Muntins
Stile
Inactive side
Threshold and sill
Rain drip
French door

Classic French door ensemble brings light, view, and spring breezes into a bedroom suite. This design combines stock wood unit, overhead fixed arch, and flanking casements.

ARCHITECT: RICHARD DODD & ASSOCIATES

Patio doors come in two basic styles: hinged and sliding. Classic French doors (left) open up to sunny garden; sliders (bottom) combine elegant styling with space efficiency. "True" divided lights (above), available for either door type, have inside and outside grilles; internal foam strips divide double glazing, too.

Patio doors are available with glazing options similar to those of modern windows (see pages 72-73). Because of the expanses of glass, it's even more critical here. Low-e glazing can prevent heat absorption, trap existing heat, and prevent fading. Double glazing not only adds energy efficiency but allows internal devices such as shades or blinds (see page 73). Patio door glazing must be tempered or laminated.

Hinged and sliding units come either prehung or as separates (you add jambs, hardware, locks, and weatherstripping). Beware: although you may find great buys on separates, it's a very tough job installing these and making them truly weathertight.

Most prehung units are placed into the rough opening from outside, then secured through exterior trim, nailing fins, or through the jambs into surrounding framing. Some models come with an adjustable sill, making installation simpler. Be sure that the sill level is 1 inch or more above an outside deck or patio to prevent water from seeping back under the door unit. Ideally, the exterior should slope slightly away from the house, at least ¼ inch per foot.

Check the Options

Ask about options such as shades, mini blinds, and hardware. Can shades be integrated into double-glazed panels? Are handles and locks extra? Are auxiliary locks or hardware available? Be sure that the screen and other accessories do not intrude on the view you are striving to create.

As with windows, you'll have options for divided lights to match your home's architecture. Grilles (see page 9) snap onto inside panes, adhere to both front and back, or slip inside the matching panes of double-glazed doors. So-called true divided lights are divided inside the glass as well as out. These have the look of individual panes, without the traditional cold air and leaks.

Sleek, sturdy French doors, built from steel, bring light and access to a contemporary kitchen. Brass cremone bolts are not only beautiful; they also help secure narrow door stiles.

DESIGN: ER. OSBURN DESIGN

INTERIOR DOORS

Most interior doors are scaled-down versions of their exterior counterparts (see pages 80–85). But indoors, you have more freedom: you won't need to worry about wind and weather whistling through not-so-tight seams, and security is a lesser issue.

The choices in both stock and custom doors are many. Swinging doors, sliding doors, bifolds, and pocket doors offer additional avenues away from the bland hollow-core door. For additional ideas see pages 62–65.

Shopping for Doors

Like exterior models, you'll find interior doors at lumberyards, home centers, and door specialty suppliers. Home centers allow you to wander around and get your hands on doors, but with less guidance and sometimes spotty selection. Door specialists can offer extra selection and service in exchange for slightly higher prices. Or commission a custom woodworker to create a one-of-a-kind design.

A potpourri of stock interior doors includes, from left to right: ten-light fir door; classic frame-and-panel model; louvered pine bifold; and hardboard-skinned, hollow-core flush door.

DOORS COURTESY OF ALLWOOD DOOR COMPANY

Construction Basics

Wood still takes center stage indoors, but surface veneers and glass panels both thicken the plot. Like exterior doors, the two basic interior door types are flush and panel.

Hollow-core flush doors are synonymous with modern construction. Rap on one with your fist. The hollow sound you get is no illusion: it's essentially an empty sandwich (see drawing at right), with thin front and back veneers over a honeycomb of corrugated cardboard or a gridwork of wood blocks, particle board, or rigid board insulation. A frame of solid lumber or lumber-core plywood holds the shape and allows cutting and planing the door to exact fit.

Flush door "skins" are typically lauan or birch, though you can find—or special-order—a variety of other, more exotic hardwood veneers. Pre-primed hardboard skins are becoming popular where paint is the final finish. You can also buy simulated panel designs fashioned from hardboard and applied moldings.

Panel doors evoke tradition and style and are making a comeback. Typically, solid-lumber rails and stiles frame raised or flat panels, either edge-joined solid lumber or hardwood plywood. Panels may be replaced by one or more glass lights. (For, example, a *six-light* door has six interior panes of glass.)

Another style for custom doors is the batten door: edge-joined solid lumber that's braced across the back with either horizontal or diagonal cross-braces. Bevels or chamfers along board edges create surface interest and mask slight joint defects. Batten designs are heavy, and there can be considerable seasonal wood movement. Beware: batten doors made from wide boards (over 6 inches or so) tend to warp.

Other Options

Pocket doors, sliding bypass doors, bifolds, and accordion doors are also found at home centers and lumberyards. You can buy most of these as

Interior Door Details

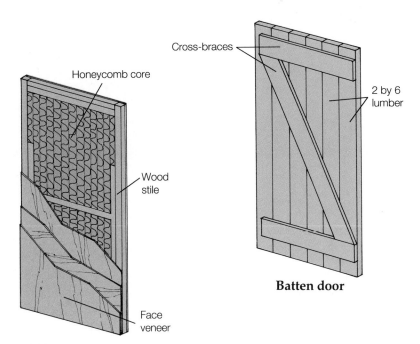

Hollow-core door

Batten door

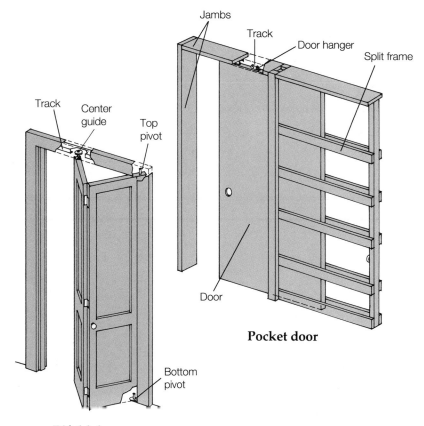

Bifold door

Pocket door

separates or as kits—with or without the hardware that goes with them. Ask about the best hardware for your situation, and find out how easy it is to install and adjust. As with any doors, you'll need to know your rough opening size to pick tracks or accessories.

Interior Door Hardware

Interior locksets reflect the basic types of exterior locks (see pages 84-85). Most modern homes have a variation on the cylindrical or tubular theme. Interior sets without locks are known as passage locks and are intended for passageways where privacy is not a problem. For bedrooms, baths, and other personal spaces, consider privacy locks: these have a locking button on the inside but can be easily opened with a key, screwdriver, or paper clip in an emergency.

The mortise locksets often found in older homes are known as "iron-key" locksets because of the old-fashioned iron keys used to operate the locking mechanism. You'll also find a whole slew of levers, latches, and pulls at your locksmith or door hardware specialist.

When lockset shopping, you'll need to know door thickness, the width of the stile, and the backset or distance from the door edge to the center of the knob hole. You'll also need to know if it's a left-hand or right-hand door. Door hand is determined from the hallway or, in a passage door, the side where the hinges don't show.

There's no rule against novel interior door shapes and colors. Arched panel doors (top) offer one alternative: these narrow units connect the kitchen and adjacent dining room. A decorative stained glass door (right) glows from the light of a wine cellar beyond.

ARCHITECT: MORIMOTO ARCHITECTS

ARCHITECT: CHURCHILL & HAMBELTON ARCHITECTS

Glazed bifold doors partition off a circular sun-room from inside living spaces. The design allows welcome light to penetrate into the main house, while sealing off the room on cold, foggy days.

Batten doors are built from edge-joined 2 by 6 fir boards; they're secured to cross-braces behind with capped wooden dowels. Penetrating oil provides a clear, glowing finish.

A SHOPPER'S GUIDE **93**

INFORMATION SOURCES

Whether you're shopping for windows or doors or working with an architect or designer to create custom solutions, you'll find a wealth of ideas and information in brochures offered by the manufacturers and associations listed here. They can also direct you to local outlets and distributors. The addresses and phone numbers in this list are accurate as of press time.

    The Yellow Pages of your telephone directory can also help you locate window and door showrooms, home centers, contractors, designers, architects, and other manufacturers and associations near you.

THE PELLA WINDOW STORE

DOORS & WINDOWS

American Architectural Manufacturers Association
1540 East Dundee Road,
Suite 310
Palatine, IL 60067
708-202-1350
(Aluminum windows)

Andersen Windows, Inc.
2001 Ruppman Plaza
Peoria, IL 61614
800-426-4261

Feather River Door
98296 Midway
Durham, CA 95938
916-895-0752

Hurd Millwork Company
575 South Whelen Avenue
Medford, WI 54451
800-223-4873

Kolbe & Kolbe Millwork Co., Inc.
1323 S. Eleventh Avenue
Wausau, WI 54401-5998
715-842-5666

Marvin Windows
PO Box 100
Warroad, MN 56763
800-346-5128

Milgard
PO Box 11368
Tacoma, WA 98411
800-MILGARD

National Wood Window and Door Association
1400 E. Touhy Avenue
Des Plaines, IL 60018
708-299-5200

Pella/Rolscreen
102 Main Street
Pella, IA 50219
800-524-3700

Pozzi Window Company
PO Box 5249
Bend, OR 97708
800-821-1016

Simpson Door Company
900 Fourth Avenue
Seattle, WA 98164
206-292-5000

Stanley Door Systems Division of The Stanley Works
1225 East Maple
Troy, MI 48084
(Steel doors)

Torrance Steel Window Co., Inc.
1819 Abalone Avenue
Torrance, CA 90501
310-328-9181

Vinyl Window and Door Institute
355 Lexington Avenue
New York, NY 10017
212-351-5400

Weather Shield Windows & Doors
PO Box 309
Medford, WI 54451
800-477-6808

Wenco Windows
Box 1248
Mount Vernon, OH 43050
800-458-9128

GLASS

National Glass Association
8200 Greensboro Drive
McLean, VA 22102
703-442-4890

Southwall Technologies
1029 Corporation Way
Palo Alto, CA 94303
415-962-0182

GLASS BLOCKS

Glashaus Inc.
Weck Glass Blocks
415 West Golf Road, Suite 13
Arlington Heights, IL 60005
708-640-6910

New High Glass
Iperfan Glass Blocks
12713 S.W. 125th Avenue
Miami, FL 33186
305-232-0840

Pittsburgh Corning
800 Presque Isle Drive
Pittsburgh, PA 15239
800-624-2120

LOCKSETS

Baldwin Hardware Corporation
841 E. Myomissing Boulevard
Reading, PA 19612
215-777-7811

Kwikset Corporation
516 E. Santa Ana St.
Anaheim, CA 92803
800-854-3151

SKYLIGHTS

Andersen Windows, Inc.
See DOORS & WINDOWS

Marvin Windows
See DOORS & WINDOWS

O'Keeffe's Inc.
75 Williams Avenue
San Francisco, CA 94124
800-227-3305

Pella/Rolscreen
See DOORS & WINDOWS

Rollamatic Roofs, Inc.
1441 Yosemite Ave.
San Francisco, CA 94124
(Retractable Skylights)

Velux-America Inc.
PO Box 5001
Greenwood, SC 29648
800-88-VELUX

Wenco Windows
See DOORS & WINDOWS

SUN-ROOMS

Four Seasons Sunrooms
5005 Veterans Memorial
Highway, Dept. UN6
Holbrook, NY 11741
800-368-7732

Lindal Cedar SunRooms
PO Box 24426, Dept. SA
Seattle, WA 98124
206-725-0900

WINDOW FILMS

Gila Energy Products
6615 West Boston Street
Chandler, AZ 85226
800-528-0481

Solar Gard International, Inc.
10801 75th Street North
Largo, FL 34647
800-282-9031

3M Company/Construction Markets
Building 225-4S-08
3M Center
St. Paul, MN 55144
800-328-1684

WINDOW SCREENS

Insect Screening Weavers Association
PO Box 1018
Ossining, NY 10562
914-962-9052
(Insect and solar screening)

Screen Manufacturers Association
3950 Lake Shore Drive
Suite 502-A
Chicago, IL 60613
312-525-2644
(Insect and solar screening)

INDEX

Boldface numbers refer to
photographs.